"Scott Aniol's book contributes to severa
an insightful critique of the Missional (
the current discussion about Christianity and culture, and offers a
direction for shaping worship in local congregations. The book is an important defense of conservative Christianity that manages to remain charitable
in the face of significant disagreements. Aniol's work should be required
reading for every course in ecclesiology, missiology, and liturgics."

—Kevin T. Bauder
Research Professor,
Central Baptist Theological Seminary of Minneapolis

"In seeking to be biblical yet missional in worship, is your church finding
it difficult to traverse the narrows between the Scylla of irrelevancy on the
one side, and the Charybdis of cultural captivity on the other? With the
wisdom and foresight of a skillful navigator, Scott Aniol points the way
forward through a sophisticated examination of the emerging movement
that has transformed many evangelical churches. Aniol contributes significantly to the contemporary discussion because he has a head surrendered
to the Word of God and a heart fully dedicated to speaking the gospel to
contemporary culture. This book will reset the discussion concerning what
it means to worship God with missional force and scriptural fidelity."

—Malcolm B. Yarnell III
Professor of Systematic Theology,
Southwestern Baptist Theological Seminary

"Sacred cows usually make poor hamburgers, but Dr. Aniol's book serves
up tasty ones by addressing issues that have become twenty-first-century sacred cows, namely missional terms, values, and attitudes that one critiques
only at great peril. Aniol does so carefully, with the skill of a surgeon, using
a biblically balanced scalpel to address emergent church challenges and sets
forth insightful correctives. He engages cultural concerns within the set of
the larger issues of contextualization in the disciplines of missiology and
cross-cultural communication of the gospel. This is a must read for those
engaged in analysis of worship styles and missiology alike."

—Keith Eitel
Professor of Missions & World Christian Studies,
Roy Fish School of Evangelism & Missions

"Scott Aniol's *By the Waters of Babylon* carefully assesses the nature of culture and worship with freshness and from a biblical base. Many will not agree with his conclusions, but no one engaged seriously in worship should fail to read this monograph. Clever, thought provoking, biblical, and firm, Aniol's perspective is profoundly relevant to our churches today."

—Paige Patterson
President, Southwestern Baptist Theological Seminary

"In a day when cultural relativism has gripped the thinking of the church, we need Scott Aniol's reminder that God is not only a culture maker but also a culture changer. I thank God for a book that exposes the myth of cultural neutrality, explains the wrong thinking that leads to it, and calls the church to embrace what he calls a "sanctificationist approach to culture." I heartily recommend Aniol's timely and articulate challenge to the popular versions of syncretistic contextualizing of worship that are so harming the church today. I pray that we will heed his appeal and return to worship that is regulated by scripture alone."

—Scott T. Brown
Pastor, Hope Baptist Church
President, National Center for Family Integrated Churches

"Dr. Aniol offers a groundbreaking treatment of the historical and philosophical underpinnings of Christian worship in the twenty-first century, integrating the themes of culture, mission, contextualization, and song for the post-Christian church. The research reflected here is of timeless value, and I expect to refer to it for decades to come."

—Mark Snoeberger
Professor of Systematic Theology, Detroit Baptist Theological Seminary.

By the Waters of Babylon

WORSHIP IN A POST-CHRISTIAN CULTURE

SCOTT ANIOL

Kregel
Ministry

Published by Kregel Publications, a division of Kregel, Inc., 2450 Oak Industrial Dr. NE, Grand Rapids, MI 49505-6020.

The Greek font GraecaU is available from www.linguistsoftware.com/lgku.htm, +1-425-775-1130.

Library of Congress Cataloging-in-Publication Data
Aniol, Scott.
 By the waters of Babylon : worship in a post-Christian culture / Scott Aniol.
 pages cm
 Includes bibliographical references and index.
 1. Public worship. 2. Christianity and culture. 3. Postmodernism—Religious aspects—Christianity. I. Title.
 BV15.A55 2015
 264—dc23

                                                    2014044106

ISBN 978-0-8254-4377-0

Printed in the United States of America
15 16 17 18 19 / 5 4 3 2 1

CONTENTS

FOREWORD

by T. David Gordon

The surprising acrimony that sometimes attended the "worship wars" of the last several decades suggested that we were talking past each other; that what we were talking about was somehow the tip of a larger, undiscussed iceberg beneath the surface. Almost all of us who have written about it have encountered opponents who misrepresented us substantially, if not entirely—not because they intended to do so, but because there are and were blindspots in the conversation, omissions that made it very difficult to hear what people actually were and were not saying. In this volume, Scott Aniol introduces us to the iceberg beneath the surface.

On first glance, some readers will wonder why a book about worship includes a discussion of the distinction between "emerging," "emergent," and "missional" churches. But Aniol demonstrates convincingly that behind these labels are different understandings not only of the relative priority of worship and mission, but even more profoundly different understandings of "culture" and cultural forms/norms. The first six chapters discuss these matters clearly, fairly, thoroughly, and judiciously; even readers who resolve some of the matters differently than the author will agree that he has represented their view justly, and has evaluated it dispassionately. The book would be valuable for these six chapters alone; and they would be useful as an introduction to cultural analysis and aesthetics on their own merits.

In these first six chapters, Aniol challenges the notion of cultural neutrality, a notion upon which much of contemporary Christian worship depends. He rightly argues that if individual sinners sometimes do unholy things, groups of such individual sinners also sometimes do unholy things, and what we call "culture" is merely the behavior that characterizes such groups of individuals. While of course God's original created order was/is "good," the works of rebellious sinners are not always good; and therefore God's works and ours should not be confused: "Wolters fails to distinguish between God's creation and man's creation. He often conflates the two categories, equating the intrinsic goodness of God's handiwork with what mankind produces" (79). In the sixth chapter, Aniol presents a lucid, biblical, alternative to false, secular understandings of culture.

The remaining five chapters present a biblical theology of worship as a gathering/meeting of God's people in His presence, by His invitation, according to His precepts, through the redemptive work of His Son. These chapters comprehend a survey of the entire biblical understanding of worship—from the original state of innocence to the consummated state in the life to come, indicating both the similarities and differences in the major moments of redemptive history along the way. In these chapters, Aniol presents a cogent argument that mission serves the greater value of worship; not the other way around. He also suggests in these chapters that Christian worship, far from imitating secular/unholy cultures' supposedly neutral habits, establishes and nurtures a holy culture, that even in its present imperfection anticipates the coming holy culture in its consummated state.

The subtitle of the book—Worship in a Post-Christian Culture—not only concurs in employing what may be a more accurate understanding of our moment than "post-modern"; it also gently suggests that we would be ill-advised to conform our liturgy to any merely human culture, and surely not to one that is post-Christian.

Some Goldilockses will say this book is "too much": too much discussion of culture and its impact on our assumptions about worship. Other Goldilockses will say it is "too little," too rapid a survey of both Christian concepts of culture and of Christian worship. I think it's just right; previous conversations about worship have been less likely to discuss the two in their relations to each other. A significant bibliography (pp. 185–199) and indices will assist those who desire to study either matter at greater length.

chapter 1

WE SAT DOWN AND WEPT: PROBLEMS FOR WORSHIP IN THE TWENTY-FIRST CENTURY

*By the waters of Babylon,
there we sat down and wept,
when we remembered Zion.
On the willows there
we hung up our lyres.
For there our captors
required of us songs,
and our tormentors, mirth, saying,
"Sing us one of the songs of Zion!"
How shall we sing the LORD's song
in a foreign land?*
Psalm 137:1–4

Imagine how they felt. For four hundred years, ever since King Solomon finished building the grand Temple in Jerusalem, the Israelites had enjoyed free and rich worship in their land. David had successfully defeated most of Israel's enemies, he had made all the preparations for the Temple and the worship to take place there, and under Solomon's reign the kingdom flourished.

On the day of the Temple dedication many years ago, hundreds of Levitical singers joined with 120 trumpeters in the Temple courts as they made themselves heard in unison in praise and thanksgiving to the Lord: "For he is good, for his steadfast love endures forever" (2 Chron. 5:13). And ever since then, elaborate rituals of worship according to God's instructions took place there for the benefit of all the people.

Yet false worship from the pagan nations crept into the land, and as a direct result of this terrible breach of God's law, the kingdom split in two. Even then, faithful Israelites were able to worship God freely, and regular Temple practices continued.

That all changed in the early sixth century BC. Nebuchadnezzar swept into the land, and after several defeats and deportations, he finally destroyed Jerusalem, including its magnificent Temple. The Israelites now found themselves in a strange land. They no longer had their own culture, protected from foreign influence. They no longer had the Ark of the Covenant, their altars, or their Temple. They no longer had their worship.

Imagine how they felt. How could they take up their lyres and sing the songs they once sang in the splendor of that great city? How could they worship their God according to his instructions when they didn't have the tools he required? How could they rejoice in his steadfast love when they were surrounded by their enemies? They were captives in Babylon; they had no reason to sing.

Instead, they sat down and wept.

Although the circumstances are certainly not exactly parallel, Christian worship in the West faces many of the same challenges as this tragic account of Israel's captivity. Emperor Constantine's legalization of Christianity in AD 313, and especially the establishment of Nicene Christianity as the state religion of the Roman Empire by Theodosius I in 380, created the conditions for what has come to be called Christendom—the union of church and state in the West such that Christianity and the West became almost synonymous. In fact, many of these early religious leaders envisioned Christendom as the New Israel, erecting ornate sanctuaries and altars, establishing a priesthood, and developing elaborate worship liturgies reminiscent of the Hebrew worship of old.

This situation persisted for hundreds of years, and while it was theologically problematic and led to many errors that resulted in need for Reformation, in the kind providence of God it did create some benefits. The most significant of these is likely the fact that free worship of the true God was permitted and even expected across the empire. The fruit of these freedoms is particularly evident in the Reformation worship traditions. With significant theological errors confronted, Reformation traditions of various stripes were enabled to perpetuate free and open God-centered, Bible-saturated worship.

Yet once again God's people were taken captive. This time, however, the invasion was not by a pagan nation but by secular philosophies, ideas that questioned the supernatural and placed their trust fully in human autonomy and reason. These influential philosophies had begun to emerge much earlier, but during the eighteenth century they came to dominate thought in the West, putting to an end the impact Christian worship had enjoyed for hundreds of years.

The people of God once again found themselves in a strange land. But this time, many of them didn't even notice.

Such is the context for what I address in this book. By all accounts Christendom is dead, and unbiblical beliefs have progressively permeated western thought, expectations, and culture. So how should churches respond to this seismic shift in their relationship to an increasingly post-Christian culture?

This question has been answered in several different ways in recent years: First, some churches continue to practice Christendom-shaped worship and completely ignore the unbelieving world around them. Churches were lulled into passivity during Christendom since everyone attended church, and thus failure to recognize the death of Christendom has left many churches impotent in their mission to evangelize the nations.

On the other hand, some churches have recognized their need to reach unbelievers with the gospel, yet they continue to operate with Christendom methods by expecting unbelievers to come to them. The church growth movement followed this pattern by insisting that a church's primary service should be an evangelistic meeting designed to attract and meet the needs of "seekers." This perspective drew fire from some who argued that this ignores worship altogether, others who complained that believers were not discipled, and still others who claimed that this "attractional" model of evangelism just did not work.

Yet in the past twenty years a new movement has emerged in evangelical Christianity that has reshaped the conversation in subtle yet profound ways by suggesting that the two priorities of worship and mission are not separate but in fact essentially connected, subsumed under the umbrella of the mission of God. Recognizing both the death of Christendom and the biblical necessity of reaching the unbelieving world, this missional church movement has significantly altered discourse about evangelism and worship, influencing evangelical churches with both a new posture toward culture in general and a new vocabulary regarding every aspect of its existence.

Missional? Emergent? Emerging? What?

If you are an evangelical Christian, chances are you've heard the term "missional." Perhaps you've used it yourself! Yet since many different kinds of churches use the term to describe often quite divergent philosophies, the term itself can be misleading. As Alan Hirsch notes,

> However, the word *missional* has tended, over the years, to become very fluid, and it was quickly co-opted by those wishing to find new and trendy tags for what they were doing, be they missional or not. It is often used as a substitute for *seeker-sensitive, cell-group church*, or other church growth concepts, thus obscuring its original meaning.[1]

As a result, many different groups have adopted the term even though they may share little more with each other than a desire to reach the lost.

A second and related challenge is that the idea of *missional* is strongly associated with the infamous "emergent church" movement. While true that those in the emergent church do share with the missional church movement an impulse to engage the culture with the gospel, they do

---

1. Alan Hirsch, *The Forgotten Ways: Reactivating the Missional Church* (Grand Rapids: Brazos Press, 2009), 82. Emphasis original.

not necessarily share a common definition of gospel. For example, Mark Driscoll, an early emergent leader who has since repudiated what he sees as doctrinal heterodoxy in the movement,[2] is quick to distinguish between *emerging* and *emergent:*

> *The emerging church* is a broad term referring to a wide variety of evangelicals seeking to be the missional church. In contrast, *Emergent* is an organization promoting a more theologically liberal and non-evangelical version of the missional church that often does not even meet the definition of a church. . . .[3]

He acknowledges the confusion with the terms, however, which reveals the connection between *emerging, emergent,* and *missional:*

> Over the years, I and others have attempted to explain the difference between the emerging church and the Emergent Village (or emergent church). Despite our best efforts, the terms are so similar that they understandably cause confusion for those unfamiliar with them. Because of this confusion and ambiguity, some have moved away from using the terms *emerging* or *emergent.* I prefer to use the term *missional* to describe those who want the church to be a missionary in culture. Some people use the term *emerging church* as synonymous with *missional church,* but for others, *emerging church* is synonymous with *emergent.* I believe that when the question on which this chapter is based [What can traditional or established churches learn from "emerging churches"?] refers to "emerging churches," it means "missional churches." The Emergent Village is a liberal subset of the missional church.[4]

A final challenge is the association of *missional* with liberal theology and the social gospel. As is clear from the history of the missional move-

---

2. Mark Driscoll, *Confessions of a Reformission Rev.: Hard Lessons from an Emerging Missional Church* (Grand Rapids: Zondervan, 2009), 21.
3. Mark Driscoll and Gerry Breshears, *Vintage Church: Timeless Truths and Timely Methods* (Wheaton, IL: Crossway, 2008), 218–19. Emphasis original.
4. Mark Driscoll, *Religion Saves: And Nine Other Misconceptions* (Wheaton, IL: Crossway, 2009), 210. Emphasis original.

ment, this association has legitimate grounding due to the prevalence of these two theological priorities among those who initiated the ideas embedded in *missional*. However, leaders in the conservative evangelical missional church movement explicitly repudiate what they consider unbiblical extensions of the missional impulse, including a redefinition of gospel that limits it to social action only.

So allow me to define what I mean by "missional" in this book. My focus is primarily on the conservative evangelical North American missional church movement that traces its philosophy to Lesslie Newbigin and the Gospel and Our Culture Network.

In order to clarify definitions and distinguish themselves from other groups that claim the title of "missional," several conservative evangelical missional leaders joined forces in April of 2011 to frame a "Missional Manifesto" with the purpose of articulating core ideas underlying the term "missional" and urging evangelicals to live in light of these ideas.[5] The framers of this document are Ed Stetzer, Alan Hirsch, Tim Keller, Dan Kimball, Eric Mason, J. D. Greear, Craig Ott, Linda Bergquist, Philip Nation, and Brad Andrews. When I talk about being "missional" in this book, I am referring primarily to the manifestation of missional ideas represented by groups who identify with the doctrinal core and missional characteristics of this Missional Manifesto.

Is the Missional Answer Right?

Missional ideas have come to saturate almost every sphere of evangelicalism in recent years. For example, the use of the term *missional*, as opposed to *missions* or *missionary*, is growing quickly across various evangelical groups. David Bosch wrote in 1991, "Since the 1950s there has been a remarkable escalation in the use of the word 'mission' among Christians,"[6] and this has only grown since then. Increasing numbers of churches, denominations, seminaries, and mission agencies use the term and explicitly adopt its core ideas. Even churches that do not use missional terminology evidence distinctive characteristics of the movement.

---

5. http://www.missionalmanifesto.com; accessed October 4, 2014.
6. David Bosch, *Transforming Mission: Paradigm Shifts in Theology of Mission* (Maryknoll, NY: Orbis Books, 1991), 1.

These missional ideas impact a number of aspects of church life and ministry, not the least of which is worship. Many church leaders today advocate allowing a missional impulse to drive all aspects of a church's worship including goals, structure, format, and musical style. In an attempt to squelch the fires of the worship wars, evangelical worship leaders call for worship rooted in the mission of God to the world. Part of the fuel for the wars is the constantly changing culture and a relentless tension between allowing the Bible to govern a church's worship and a church's calling to reach the increasingly pagan world for Christ. Recognizing the postmodern, post-Christian nature of the North American context, worship leaders are asking, "What worship forms will best accomplish God's mission in our culture?"

I believe that the missional church movement has had some positive impact upon worship in the evangelical church. As we shall see, it has caused churches to give much more careful consideration to how much of its worship methodology has been shaped by culture rather than Scripture and how it can recover believers' worship that had been lost in the church growth movement's evangelistic restructuring, while nevertheless making worship intelligible to unbelievers.

Yet in its noble ambition to recover truly missional worship, the missional church movement has failed to recognize how its own understanding of both worship and culture has been shaped by the Christendom and Enlightenment models it repudiates. Therefore, it is my contention that the full correction of errors regarding worship and evangelism that missional advocates rightly identify requires more careful study of culture and worship and their relation to evangelism from a biblical perspective.

The purpose of this book is to answer the question I posed earlier: How should churches today worship considering the increasingly pagan culture around them *and* their biblical mandate to reach that culture with the gospel of Jesus Christ?

I believe that the missional church movement has correctly identified many of the issues involved in answering this question, and their own answer has been perhaps the most influential recently. However, I'm convinced that their answer has some significant problems that, if left unchallenged, will result in churches both failing to worship God according to Scripture and losing their ability to faithfully accomplish the mission he has given to them.

For these reasons, the book begins with a focus on missional theology in order to evaluate its impact upon evangelical worship theology and practice in North America. After ascertaining common principles guiding missional worship today, I assess the strengths of this worship development and reveal weaknesses in three primary areas: its view of the nature of culture, the posture of contextualization, and the relationship between worship and evangelism.

The Plan

In order to get at the heart of this important question, I will begin by providing a brief history of the missional church movement, and then I will summarize and explain the theological distinctives that drive its practice. I will then show specifically how missional thinking impacts worship philosophy and practice by looking at what these authors themselves say about how churches should worship and how worship relates to mission.

This will lead to an extended discussion of one of the issues most relevant to this discussion: culture. Since how we worship and how we present the gospel necessarily involve culture, understanding what culture is and the proper Christian approach to culture is of utmost importance. The missional church movement's practice of worship flows from a particular philosophy of culture, and so I will evaluate that perspective and offer what I believe to be a more biblically faithful alternative.

I will then be prepared to offer my answer to the question under consideration. I will biblically define both worship and mission, spend some time exploring the nature and importance of the cultural forms we use in worship, and articulate an understanding of biblical authority over worship that relies on its guidance—rather than the surrounding culture—to shape worship practice.

My desire is to help pastors and other interested Christians wrestle through this critical issue of the relationship between Christian worship and evangelistic witness, especially in the context of an increasingly hostile culture. My goal in this book is to convince you that biblically regulated, gospel-shaped corporate worship that communicates God's truth through appropriate cultural forms will actually have the most missional impact in a post-Christian context.

chapter 2

EXILE IN BABYLON:

MISSIONAL ANSWERS TO

POST-CHRISTENDOM MINISTRY

Why should the nations say,
"Where is their God?"
Our God is in the heavens;
he does all that he pleases.
Psalm 115:2–3

The church today is in captivity, but many Christians don't realize it. We still live in a Christian nation, don't we? There isn't any overt paganism around us, is there?

One of the most significant contributions of missional thinking is that it identifies that this perspective fails to recognize the post-Christian nature of the West. The biblical values that once did govern the civilization have been replaced with secularist philosophies, and this has impacted all aspects of the public sphere. Missional authors have rightly advocated viewing our own context as a mission field.

In order to understand the driving impulses behind the North American evangelical missional church movement, I want to begin with a brief survey of the history of ideas embedded in *missional*. The most thorough analysis of the history of this movement is David Bosch's *Transforming Mission: Paradigm Shifts in Theology of Mission*, which I will simply summarize here.

A Brief History of the Missional Church Movement

Ecumenical Roots

Contemporary missional thinking began within the larger ecumenical missions debates in the early twentieth century. Critics of standard missionary methods argued that current foreign missions models were too tied to Western cultural superiority and undermined indigenous cultural forms. The earliest roots of this new missional thinking can be traced to the meetings of the International Missionary Council (IMC), in which debates about the relationship between church and "mission" took place. The first significant, influential shift in thinking occurred in the 1938 meeting in Tambaram, India. Out of this meeting came one of the earliest articulations of indigenization and connecting mission with church. The Council refocused missions toward God's sending the church and emphasized the importance of indigenous ministry. The 1952 Willingen meeting built on these ideas and first rooted both mission and church in the *missio Dei*—the mission of God. Instead of missions being seen as an activity of the church, the church was now considered a part of God's mission on earth. The conclusion reached at the meeting was that,

> God's salvific work precedes both the church and mission. We should not subordinate mission to the church nor the church to mission; both should, rather, be taken up into the *missio Dei*, which now became the overarching concept. The *missio Dei* institutes the *missiones ecclesiae*.[1]

A key leader during this period was Johannes Hoekendijk (1912–1975), who defined *missio Dei* as something larger than just the church, redefining the concept of mission for the ecumenical church. He extended missions beyond merely evangelism into broader works, especially social

---

1. Bosch, *Transforming Mission*, 370.

justice. When the IMC merged with the World Council of Churches in 1961, this "missional" thinking spread to the degree that even the Roman Catholic Church adopted missional language in Vatican II. Evangelicals initially rejected this redefinition of Christian mission, believing that it led to a secularizing of missionary activity to the degree that gospel witness was all but lost in the process; "mission" had been redefined as God's work to restore the world, and therefore the church's task was to contribute to the mission through social acts.

Conservative Evangelical Propagation

While conservative evangelicals originally repudiated an idea of *missio Dei* that led to an exclusively social gospel, nevertheless the writings and even language of these early thinkers influenced later evangelical discussion of mission, specifically the broader idea of *missio Dei*. John Stott (1921–2011) recovered some of the evangelical emphasis in mission by asserting in 1975 that *missio Dei* necessarily included both social action *and* evangelism.[2] Stott's protégé, Christopher Wright, later built on his predecessor's ideas by broadening the mission of God to all his saving acts in history.[3]

One of the influential leaders at Willingen was Lesslie Newbigin (1909–1998), an Anglican missionary to India. Newbigin was instrumental in formulating the position documents that resulted from the meeting, but his greatest impact upon the later missional church movement, especially in North America, came after he retired from missionary work and returned to Great Britain in 1974. Newbigin noticed upon his return that Western civilization now required the same kind of cross-cultural ministry that he advocated at Willingen and that he attempted while a missionary abroad. Newbigin recognized that the West had become "post-Christian" and pluralistic, now legitimately earning it the moniker of "pagan," and he urged the church in the West to endeavor for a "genuine missionary encounter" with its culture.[4] He began asking the penetrating question,

---

2. John R. W. Stott, *Christian Mission in the Modern World* (Downers Grove, IL: InterVarsity Press, 1975), 23.
3. Christopher Wright, *The Mission of God: Unlocking the Bible's Grand Narrative* (Downers Grove, IL: IVP Academic, 2006).
4. Lesslie Newbigin, *The Other Side of 1984: Questions for the Churches* (Geneva: World Council of Churches, 1983), 31.

"What would be involved in a missionary encounter between the gospel and this whole way of perceiving, thinking, and living that we call 'modern Western Culture'?"[5] Michael Goheen summarizes the impact of Newbigin's writings on missional ideology: "It is precisely the missionary ecclesiology developed by Newbigin that has been foundational for and formative of both his work within the ecumenical movement and his call for a missionary encounter with western culture."[6]

Newbigin's influence spread to North America in the 1980s, leading to the formation of the Gospel and our Culture Network (GOCN) under the leadership of George Hunsberger. According to Hunsberger,

> The GOCN is a collaborative effort that focuses on three things: (1) a cultural and social analysis of our North American setting; (2) theological reflection on the question, what is the gospel that addresses us in our setting? and (3) the renewal of the church and its missional identity in our setting.[7]

The most notable missional writer from the GOCN was Darrell Guder, whose influential *Missional Church* provided the material for an explosion of other thinking and writing on the subject. Hunsberger contributed to this work, and other contributing authors such as Alan J. Roxburgh and Craig Van Gelder have proven to be influential missional leaders in their own right.

Contemporary Practitioners

Perhaps the most important group to trace because of its direct impact upon the life of evangelical churches is those who write and teach on a more practical level, offering explanation and application of missional ideas for the contemporary church. This group includes evangelical pastors, church planters, and seminary professors who have been influenced to some degree by the missional theologians of the past and

---

5. Lesslie Newbigin, *Foolishness to the Greeks: The Gospel and Western Culture* (Grand Rapids: Wm. B. Eerdmans, 1986), 1.
6. Michael Goheen, "'As The Father Has Sent Me, I Am Sending You': Lesslie Newbigin's Missionary Ecclesiology" (PhD diss., Utrecht University, 2002), 22.
7. George Hunsberger, *The Church Between Gospel and Culture: The Emerging Mission in North America* (Grand Rapids: Wm. B. Eerdmans, 1996), 290.

who seek to apply at least the core ideas propagated by these theologians to practical church context.

Among the practical writers/theologians, Ed Stetzer and Alan Hirsch have probably done more to spread missional ideas to the average local church planter and pastor than anyone else. Ed Stetzer is president of LifeWay Research and missiologist in residence at LifeWay Christian Resources in Nashville, Tennessee. He has planted several churches and written or edited a number of books on missiology in general and the missional church specifically, and he was the driving force behind the Missional Manifesto. Another framer of the Missional Manifesto, Alan Hirsch is a South African-born church planter and the founding Director of Forge Mission Training Network. His books and teaching have also been influential in spreading a practical application of missional ideas.

Tim Keller and Mark Driscoll stand out as notable pastors who actively articulate missional thinking. Tim Keller is the founding pastor of Redeemer Presbyterian Church in New York City, one of the co-founders of The Gospel Coalition, and a framer of the Missional Manifesto. Mark Driscoll founded Mars Hill Church in Seattle, Washington, as well as the Acts 29 church planting network, which is explicitly missional in its philosophy. Both Keller and Driscoll have done more teaching on being missional than formal writing, but their influence is no less.

A Theological Survey of the Missional Church Movement

Understanding the impact of the missional church movement upon evangelical worship first requires a grasp of the fundamental principles that characterize the movement. Each of these ideas applies directly to worship philosophy.

Missionary Imperative

The first principle that drives the missional church is what it considers the biblically mandated missionary imperative. While evangelical churches have traditionally considered evangelism and missions a critical reason for their existence, the missional church understands such an emphasis as not just one ministry among many but as the overarching idea of what it means to be a church.

Missio Dei. Missional authors are critical of what they call an "ecclesiocentric understanding of mission" that has so characterized the church in the West. Rather, they have sought to reclaim a theocentric vision for mission by defining mission, not as part of the church's work, but as the very purpose of God himself throughout history and into which the church's work fits. Newbigin was instrumental in this shift in thinking. Without using the term *missio Dei*, he expressed its essence when he wrote,

> The missionary movement of which we are part has its source in the triune God himself. Out of the depths of his love for us, the Father has sent forth his own beloved Son to reconcile all things to Himself, that we and all men might, through the Spirit, be made one in him with the Father in that perfect love which is the very nature of God.[8]

Guder and others in the GOCN continued to develop this theme, re-centering mission in its God-centered purpose:

> The subtle assumption of much Western mission was that the church's missionary mandate lay not only in forming the church of Jesus Christ, but in shaping the Christian communities that it birthed in the image of the church of western European culture. This ecclesiocentric understanding of mission has been replaced in this century by a profoundly theocentric reconceptualization of Christian mission. We have come to see that mission is not merely an activity of the church. Rather, mission is the result of God's initiative, rooted in God's purpose to restore and heal creation. "Mission" means "sending," and it is the central biblical theme describing the purpose of God's action in human history. God's mission began with the call of Israel to receive God's blessings in order to be a blessing to the nations. God's mission unfolded in the mission of God's people across the centuries recorded in Scripture, and it reached its revelatory climax in the incarnation of God's work

---

8. Norman Goodall, ed., *Missions Under the Cross: Addresses Delivered at the Enlarged Meeting of the Committee of the International Missionary Council at Willingen, in Germany, 1952; with Statements Issued by the Meeting* (London: Edinburgh House Press, 1953), 189.

of salvation in Jesus ministering, crucified, and resurrected. God's mission continued then in the sending of the Spirit to call forth and empower the church as the witness of churches in every culture to the gospel of Jesus Christ, and it moves toward the promised consummation of God's salvation in the *eschaton* ("last" or "final day").[9]

This refocus is important for missional thinking because it is inherently God-centered rather than church-centered or individual-centered. Missional advocates argue that God has been at work accomplishing his mission for mankind since the beginning of human history, and the purposes of his people fit within that mission.

The Church as Sent. Flowing naturally from the idea that God has an overarching mission for mankind, thus rendering that mission God-centered, is the assertion that the church, as one component of that mission, is sent by God to help accomplish the mission. Newbigin saw a natural flow from the idea that mission begins with God's purpose of reconciling the world to himself to the truth that the church is part of that mission:

> We who have been chosen in Christ, reconciled to God through him, made members of his Body, sharers in his Spirit, and heirs through hope of his Kingdom, are by these very facts committed to full participation in his mission to the world. That by which the Church receives its existence is that by which it is also given its world-mission. "As the Father has sent me, even so send I you."[10]

DuBose explains how the very idea of mission is inherently one of sending:

> Why limit the meaning of mission to sending? The answer is because that is what mission means. If we are to capture this essential idea, we must be guided by the discipline of that idea. Since mission and sending have essentially the same meaning, we look for its meaning in the message it conveys in Scripture

---

9. Darrell Guder, *Missional Church: A Vision for the Sending of the Church in North America* (Grand Rapids: Wm. B. Eerdmans, 1998), 4. Emphasis original.
10. Goodall, *Missions Under the Cross*, 189.

just as we look for the meaning of covenant, kingdom, grace
or any other biblical concept through that precise language, at
least at the outset.[11]

Missional proponents will suggest that this conception is a subtle yet
radical shift from the way missions has been viewed in the past. Previ-
ously, the church considered missions to be one of its several ministries;
now, missions is not a component of the church, the church is part of the
mission of God. As Hirsch succinctly states, "The church must follow
mission."[12] Guder explains, "In particular, we have begun to see that the
church of Jesus Christ is not the purpose or goal of the gospel, but rather
its instrument and witness."[13]

This is inherently communicated in the key definitions of *mission* or
missional formulated by missional proponents. Consider, for example,
Alan Hirsch's definition:

> So a working definition of missional church is a community of
> God's people that defines itself, and organizes itself around, its
> real purpose of being an agent of God's mission in the world. In
> other words, the church's true and authentic organizing principle
> is mission. When the church is in mission, it is the true church.
> The church itself is not only a product of that mission but is obli-
> gated and destined to extend it by whatever means possible. The
> mission of God flows directly through every believer and every
> community of faith adheres to Jesus. To obstruct this is to block
> God's purpose in and through his people.[14]

In other words, if a church does not understand its essence as being rooted in "sentness," then it is not a true church.

The idea that the church is part of mission and not the other way
around has important implications for how missional thinkers understand
the role of the church in its cultural context. God has sent the church into

---

11. Francis DuBose, *God Who Sends: A Fresh Quest for Biblical Mission* (Nashville: Broadman
Press, 1983), 25.
12. Hirsch, *The Forgotten Ways*, 143.
13. Guder, *Missional Church*, 5.
14. Hirsch, *The Forgotten Ways*, 82.

the world, and yet, according to missional authors, the Western church has mostly expected the world to come to it. This is the essence of the church growth movement, as Van Gelder explains:

> Approaching the work of the church from a very different perspective, [the church growth] movement focused on reaching persons outside the church to incorporate them into the church. To do so, it intentionally planted congregations within given social boundaries so that persons could meet Christ without having to cross cultural barriers.[15]

Proponents of missional theology are quite critical of what they call the "attractional" model of evangelism, where churches establish programs and design services to attract unbelievers so that they may encounter the gospel. Rather, the church must go out into the world.

Twenty-First-Century Western Postmodernism as Missionary Context

Understanding this missionary imperative for the church leads missional writers to ask the question, "Are twenty-first-century North American churches fulfilling their place in the mission of God?" Guder answers bluntly, "Neither the structures nor the theology of our established Western traditional churches is missional."[16] Rather, the church today is locked in the mode of what missional authors call "Christendom," pre-Enlightenment Western civilization.

The Rise of Christendom. The rise of so-called "Christendom" began with the Edict of Milan in 313 in which Roman Emperor Constantine I (272–337) declared religious toleration in the empire. The formerly persecuted Christian church now began to enjoy new-found freedom, reaching its climax in 380 when Emperor Theodosius I (347–395) made Christianity the Roman Empire's official religion. In 392 he outlawed any form of pagan worship, and the church thus became the controlling influence in the entirety of the empire.

---

15. Craig Van Gelder, "Missional Context: Understanding North American Culture," in *Missional Church: A Vision for the Sending of the Church in North America*, ed. Darrell Guder (Grand Rapids: Wm. B. Eerdmans, 1998), 73.
16. Guder, *Missional Church*, 5.

Although the church developed some serious theological and philosophical errors during this period, it nevertheless exerted a positive spiritual influence on western culture. Hirsch explains:

> For all its failings, the church, up till the time of the Enlightenment, played the overwhelmingly dominant role in the mediation of identity, meaning, purpose, and community for at least the preceding eleven centuries in the West.[17]

This had certain cultural and social benefits for the West, but with western civilization governed to a significant extent by Christianity, the church lost its missionary impulse. Church buildings became the central focus of church life; people came to the church, and therefore there was no need for the church to go to the people. As Stetzer notes,

> Until the last several years in the history of the United States, Christianity was thought to be the "American religion" even though it was not embraced by everyone or practiced with devotion that committed Christians would like. It was once perceived as part of America's ethos.[18]

The Fall of Christendom. The church enjoyed its seat of power in the West for almost 1,200 years until it was dethroned by Enlightenment philosophers. The Enlightenment "sought to establish reason over revelation through philosophy and science, eventually forcing a separation of the power of the church from that of the state."[19] Through philosophers such as René Descartes (1595–1650) and David Hume (1711–1776), human autonomy, individualism, and reason won the day, and this had earth-shattering impact upon Christianity in the public sphere. "Christianity has become a mere matter of private preference rather than that of public truth."[20] Because reason replaced faith as the controlling impulse of western culture, the church "lost its position of privilege."[21] Instead

---

17. Hirsch, *The Forgotten Ways*, 108.
18. Ed Stetzer, *Planting Missional Churches* (Nashville: Broadman & Holman, 2006), 19.
19. Hirsch, *The Forgotten Ways*, 60.
20. Ibid., 108.
21. Bosch, *Transforming Mission*, 364.

of the church being at the center of Western culture, the culture became secularized, which Hirsch describes as "that process whereby the church was taken from the center of culture (as in the Christendom period) and increasingly pushed to the margins."[22]

The fall of Christendom created a situation that was entirely foreign to a church steeped in a way of operating that had continued for eleven centuries, and according to missional writers, the effects remain to this day. What the death of Christendom means for the church today is that, just as Lesslie Newbigin noticed when he returned from India to Great Britain, the West is as much a pluralistic, "heathen" mission field as any foreign nation. As Stetzer notes,

> The end of Christendom allows the church to recognize that the gospel is distinct from Western culture. So the gospel must be addressed in fresh ways to the ever-changing population that's disassociated itself from "pseudo-Christian" roots. In other words, being missional is not just the task of taking the gospel to the "primitives" outside our borders. The new challenge is to bring the gospel to Western culture, including right here in North America, since it's become so resistant to the gospel.[23]

The State of Mission Today. Missional authors argue that churches today have failed to recognize that the Christendom era has ended. They no longer enjoy the level of influence and status they once did, but their structures, ministries, philosophies, and methods nevertheless remain the same. Mead notes,

> We are surrounded by the relics of the Christendom Paradigm, a paradigm that has largely ceased to work. [These] relics hold us hostage to the past and make it difficult to create a new paradigm that can be as compelling for the next age as the Christendom Paradigm has been for the past age.[24]

---

22. Hirsch, *The Forgotten Ways*, 108.
23. Stetzer, *Planting Missional Churches*, 19.
24. Loren Mead, *The Once and Future Church: Reinventing the Congregation for a New Mission Frontier* (Washington, DC: Alban Institute, 1991), 18.

Furthermore, churches also fail to recognize how much their methods have been shaped first by a Christendom mode of cultural engagement and second by subtle influences of post-Enlightenment thinking. In one sense, churches continue to expect the world to come to them as the church did during Christendom, and they have been scrambling for new methods to help attract unbelievers into their four walls. With the fall of Christendom, churches found themselves increasingly irrelevant; so now, desiring to maintain the same kind of power they once enjoyed, churches constantly seek after new ways to compete for the attention of the masses. Hirsch explains the problem with this posture:

> The problem for the church in this situation is that it is now forced to compete with all the other ideologies and –isms in the marketplace of religions and products for the allegiance of people, and it must do this in a way that mirrors the dynamics of the marketplace—because that is precisely the basis of how people make the countless daily choices in their lives. In the modern and the postmodern situation, the church is forced into the role of being little more than a *vendor of religious goods and services.*[25]

This is exactly why Hirsch and other missional leaders are so critical of the church growth models that make use of "attractional" methods—they are buying into consumerism—something Hirsch would argue was nurtured in Christendom:

> Church growth exponents have explicitly taught us how to market and tailor the product to suit target audiences. They told us to mimic the shopping mall, apply it to the church, and create a one-stop religious shopping experience catering to our every need. … Christendom, operating as it does in the attractional mode and run by professionals, was already susceptible to consumerism, but under the influence of contemporary church growth practice, consumerism has actually become the driving ideology of the church's ministry.[26]

---

25. Hirsch, *The Forgotten Ways*, 110. Emphasis original.
26. Ibid.

Missional leaders insist that the church growth movement attracts only older generations that still manifest remnants of a Christendom mind-set or people who have grown up in Christianity. For example, Van Gelder suggests,

> The continued drift toward the development of large, independent community churches, with their focus on user-friendly, needs oriented, market-driven models described by George Barna in *User Friendly Churches*, is in need of careful critique. While celebrating their contextual relevance, we need to be careful that we are committed in using these approaches to maintaining the integrity of both the gospel and the Christian community. These churches may just be the last version of the Christian success story within the collapsing paradigm of modernity and Christian-shaped culture.[27]

Therefore, because of their Christendom inheritance, churches, according to missional advocates, consider missions to be one of their many tasks rather than understanding their purpose to be found within the greater mission of God. Guder argues,

> One needs only to visit North American congregations to find that the church-centered approach to mission is alive and well. Congregations still tend to view missions as one of several programs of the church. Evangelism, when present, is usually defined as member recruitment at the local level and as church planting at the regional level. The sending-receiving mentality is still strong as churches collect funds and send them off to genuine mission enterprises elsewhere. Indeed, the main business of many mission committees is to determine how to spend the mission budget rather than view the entire congregational budget as an exercise in mission.[28]

---

27. Craig Van Gelder, "Defining the Center—Finding the Boundaries," in *The Church Between Gospel and Culture: The Emerging Mission in North America*, ed. George Hunsberger and Craig Van Gelder (Grand Rapids: Wm. B. Eerdmans, 1996), 45.
28. Guder, *Missional Church*, 6.

The Incarnational Mode of Mission

If the "why" of mission is the fact that God sends the church, and if the "where" of mission is post-Christendom Western culture, then for the missional advocates the "how" of mission is incarnation. By *incarnation*, missional writers mean that a truly missional church is one that is embedded in its target culture. Hirsch notes,

> Many churches have mission statements or talk about the importance of mission, but where truly missional churches differ is in their posture toward the world. A missional community sees the mission as both its originating impulse and its organizing principle. A missional community is patterned after what God has done in Jesus Christ. In the incarnation God sent his Son. Similarly, to be missional means to be sent into the world; we do not expect people to come to us. This posture differentiates a missional church from an attractional church.[29]

Of course, missional exponents adapt the term from the way in which Jesus Christ was sent—he immersed himself in the culture of humanity in order to redeem it—and this adaptation is intentional. One of the key texts for missional thinking is John 20:21: "As the Father has sent me, even so I am sending you." God has sent the church, just as he did his Son, into the world in order to redeem it, and no culture is exempt from the possibility of redemption: "All human cultures, marked as they are by the tension of being *simul creates et peccator* (simultaneously created and sinful), are honored by God as potential receivers of Christ and his calling."[30]

Contextualization. Another key idea for the missional movement that is related to the idea of incarnation is contextualization. For missional proponents, contextualization is at the heart of what it means for a church to be embedded in its target culture. In order for a church to reach its culture, the church must contextualize so that its message is intelligible to its audience. According to Newbigin, contextualization is

---

29. Alan Hirsch, "Defining Missional," *Leadership Journal*, Fall 2008, http://www.christianityto-day.com/le/2008/fall/17.20.html; accessed November 26, 2012.
30. Darrell Guder, *The Continuing Conversion of the Church* (Grand Rapids: Wm. B. Eerdmans, 2000), 84. Emphasis original.

"the placing of the gospel in the total context of a culture at a particular moment, a moment that is shaped by the past and looks to the future."[31] This is important, because as the culture moves further and further from its Christendom past, the gospel and Christendom methods will become more foreign. As Van Gelder explains,

> It is important, then, for the church to study its context carefully and to understand it. The technical term for this continuing discipline is contextualization. Since everyone lives in culture, the church's careful study of its context will help the church to translate the truth of the gospel as good news for the society to which it is sent.[32]

Missional proponents insist that churches be truly indigenous, inheriting ideas spawned in 1938 at the International Missionary Council in Tambaram:

> An indigenous church, young or old, in the East or in the West, is a church which, rooted in obedience to Christ, spontaneously uses forms of thought and modes of action natural and familiar in its own environment. Such a church arises in response to Christ's own call. The younger churches will not be unmindful of the experiences and teachings which the older churches have recorded in their confessions and liturgy. But every younger church will seek further to bear witness to the same Gospel with new tongues.[33]

Missional authors apply the indigenous principles that have characterized foreign missions for years to the North American context. Since the West is now post-Christendom, churches in the West "should reflect the full social mix of the communities they serve, if they are truly contextual."[34]

---

31. Newbigin, *Foolishness to the Greeks*, 2.
32. Van Gelder, "Missional Context," 18.
33. International Missionary Council, *The Growing Church* (London: Oxford University Press, 1939), 276.
34. Craig Van Gelder, "Missional Challenge: Understanding the Church in North America," in *Missional Church*, 70.

Not only should missional churches reflect the cultures around them, but they should also immerse themselves in the expressions of those cultures in order to understand them and use them as a bridge to the gospel. Van Gelder elaborates:

> We need to exegete ... culture in the same way the missionaries have been so good at doing with diverse tribal cultures of previously unreached people. We need to exegete ... the themes of the Rolling Stones ... , Dennis Rodman, Madonna, David Letterman, Rosanne, Seinfeld, and "Tales from the Crypt." We need to comprehend that the Spirit of the Living God is at work in these cultural expressions, preparing the hearts of men and women to receive the gospel of Jesus Christ. We have to find, in good missionary fashion, those motifs and themes that connect with the truths of the gospel. We need to learn how to proclaim, "That which you worship as unknown, I now proclaim to you." This is missionary vision at its best.[35]

Missional experts highlight primarily two passages of Scripture in support of their view of contextualization. First, they appeal to 1 Corinthians 9:19–23:

> For though I am free from all, I have made myself a servant to all, that I might win more of them. To the Jews I became as a Jew, in order to win Jews. To those under the law I became as one under the law (though not being myself under the law) that I might win those under the law. To those outside the law I became as one outside the law (not being outside the law of God but under the law of Christ) that I might win those outside the law. To the weak I became weak, that I might win the weak. I have become all things to all people, that by all means I might save some. I do it all for the sake of the gospel, that I may share with them in its blessings.

35. Craig Van Gelder, *Confident Witness—Changing World: Rediscovering the Gospel in North America* (Grand Rapids: Wm. B. Eerdmans, 1999), 14–15.

Stetzer and Putman say of this passage, "Paul is the model for us in that he made himself a slave to the preference and cultures of others, rather than a slave to his own preferences."[36] Parris comments, "Paul held deep personal convictions, yet he searched for customs and traditions with which he could sympathize in order to place himself in the position to win them to Christ."[37]

Missional exponents also often look to Paul's sermon on Mars Hill in Acts 17:16–34 as the supreme example of missional contextualization, so much so that Mark Driscoll even named his church "Mars Hill":

> When the apostle Paul stood atop Mars Hill, he proclaimed good news to a diverse people steeped in philosophy, culture, and spirituality. Mars Hill Church seeks to continue that legacy in modern-day Seattle. Our city is a place much like first-century Athens: a marketplace of ideas, a vibrant arts community, and a metropolitan hub.
>
> Our church is more than a building, an organization, a man, or a Sunday. Mars Hill Church is a group of missionaries united by a common relationship with Jesus Christ. We want to share him with Seattle by serving and loving the city and preaching the gospel like Paul: using the artifacts and language of our culture to point to Jesus.[38]

Paul's engaging of the culture of Athens in his attempt to win them to Christ serves as a model for missional churches. Stetzer and Putman comment, "The culture of the hearer impacted his missional methods,"[39] and Van Gelder notes that "Paul argued philosophy with secular philosophy on secular terms."[40] A missional church will immerse itself in its culture so that it can understand and engage its culture on its own terms.

---

36. Ed Stetzer and David Putman, *Breaking the Missional Code: Your Church Can Become a Missionary in Your Community* (Nashville: Broadman & Holman, 2006), 52.
37. Stanley Glenn Parris, "Instituting a Missional Worship Style in a Local Church Developed from an Analysis of the Culture" (PhD diss., Asbury Theological Seminary, 2008), 28.
38. http://www.marshillchurch.org/newhere; accessed February 15, 2008.
39. Stetzer and Putman, *Breaking the Missional Code*, 183.
40. Craig Van Gelder, *The Missional Church and Leadership Formation: Helping Congregations Develop Leadership Capacity* (Grand Rapids: Wm. B. Eerdmans, 2009), 118.

Missional Understanding of Culture. Inherent in this insistence upon incarnation and contextualization is the idea that no aspect of culture is inherently sinful, or at very least unredeemable. Missional proponents believe that there are very few aspects of human culture that are actually sinful in and of themselves; they might cite pornography or something similar as an example of inherently sinful cultural expression, but not much else. Most of culture is neutral and may be received with open arms. Some aspects of culture may be used sinfully or have harmful baggage surrounding them, but even then they can be redeemed by Christians who take them and use them for good.

Therefore, there is a two-fold relationship with culture that exists for a missional church: a missional church seeks to engage culture and influence it while at the same time allowing its message to be shaped by culture so that it will be intelligible to the culture. Guder elaborates:

> This shaping always moves in two directions. On the one hand, the church understands that under the power of God, the gospel shapes the culture of a society—its assumptions, its perspectives, its choices. The church knows this because the gospel is always doing that to the very culture that is its own. This gives an indication of God's vision for the church's transforming impact on its context. On the other hand, because the church is incarnational, it also knows that it will always be called to express the gospel within the terms, styles, and perspectives of its social context. It will be shaped by that context, just as it will constantly challenge and shape that context. The church lives in the confidence that this ought to be so, and that it is the nature of its calling for this to be so.[41]

Yet there does seem to be somewhat of a disconnect between the missional theologians and the missional practitioners on this point. The theologians seem to emphasize the fact that culture shapes the church (especially harkening back to the ways Christendom and the Enlightenment shaped the church in the West) and warn against being shaped by culture

---

41. Guder, *Missional Church*, 15.

EXILE IN BABYLON: MISSIONAL ANSWERS TO POST-CHRISTENDOM MINISTRY

in ways that "might be compromising gospel truth."[42] Most practitioners, on the other hand, tend to minimize the possibility that any culture could shape the gospel harmfully, instead emphasizing the need for the church to engage the culture and redeem it for the gospel. For example, after acknowledging the possibility of sinful elements in culture, Driscoll nevertheless insists,

> As we engage culture, we must watch films, listen to music, read books, watch television, shop at stores, and engage in other activities as theologians and missionaries filled with wisdom and discernment, seeking to better grasp life of our Mars Hill. We do this so we can begin the transforming work of the gospel in our culture.[43]

Missional thinking has profoundly reshaped the debate about the relationship between various ministries of the church by subsuming them all under the *missio Dei*. Every one of the North American evangelical church's various priorities must fit under the priority of "sentness" and thus must both engage and be shaped by the emerging culture of twenty-first-century North America. Nothing escapes this emphasis, not even—or perhaps *especially*—the church's worship.

---

42. Van Gelder, "Missional Challenge," 18.
43. Mark Driscoll, *The Radical Reformission: Reaching Out without Selling Out* (Grand Rapids: Zondervan, 2006), 127.

chapter 3

HOW SHALL WE SING

THE LORD'S SONG

IN A FOREIGN LAND?

I was glad when they said to me,
"Let us go to the house of the LORD!"
Our feet have been standing
within your gates, O Jerusalem!
Psalm 122:1–2

Here they were in a strange land far away from their homes, and their oppressors wanted them to sing songs of Zion! The captive Israelites now faced a struggle they had never encountered before: how do they maintain their distinctiveness as God's people in worship and life while living in a different culture?

Today, Christians have to wrestle through an even more challenging dilemma since the church is not limited to one ethnic group, but to people of every race. So how do we worship God rightly in a post-Christian culture while at the same time being a witness to that culture?

Missional thinking affects every aspect of local church philosophy and methodology, and it has attempted to answer this very question regarding the relationship between worship, culture, and mission. I would like to survey what missional authors say about this important matter, note what I believe to be positive contributions, and begin a discussion of where their philosophy is biblically problematic.

Relationship of Worship to Mission

As mentioned earlier, part of the difficulty in attempting to synthesize a philosophy of missional worship is that many different groups have adopted the term *missional* to describe their approach to church ministry, not all of which ascribe to the fundamental characteristics of the missional movement. For example, while missional church advocates discussed above repudiate an attractional model of evangelism, many proponents of a seeker model of worship call themselves "missional."[1] Therefore, the discussion in this section will narrowly focus on the writings of those already discussed above (Guder, Van Gelder, Stetzer, Hirsch, Keller, Driscoll, et al.), those worship writers these men specifically quote (Morgenthaler especially), and worship writers who share the most core theological and philosophical values with these missional leaders (Kimball, the Kreiders, Townley, Wheeler, and Whaley). The framework of this section will take the shape of the discussion in the previous chapter of distinctives of the missional movement, each of which impacts the philosophy and methodology of worship.

The Missionary Imperative of Worship

First, for missional churches, worship serves mission. If the church is part of mission, not the other way around, then everything the church does, including worship, serves mission. The question is, *how* does worship serve mission? On this point, Thomas H. Schattauer presents three possible views concerning the relationship between worship and mission. The first is what he calls "Inside & Out," the view that worship serves the end of mission; it is what fuels and motivates worshipers to take their message outside the walls of the church building. In this sense, "Mission is what takes place on the outside when the gospel is proclaimed to those who have not heard or received it or . . . when the neighbor is served in acts of love and justice."

---

1. See Hirsch, *The Forgotten Ways*, 82.

He calls the second approach "Outside In," in which the central purpose of worship is to evangelize unbelievers. This would essentially characterize the contemporary church growth movement. Schattauer's final category is "Inside Out," which he considers to be the most truly missional since it "locates the liturgical assembly itself within the arena of the *missio Dei*." Worship in this view is not a means toward the end of evangelism, as with the other two, but rather fits within the larger purpose of mission. In fact, Schattauer does not see worship and mission as two separate categories, but rather "the assembly for worship is mission."[2]

Missional writers almost unanimously repudiate the second position, calling it "attractional" and citing it as the "Christendom" model of evangelism. Some missional writers do claim legitimacy for the first view, such as Guder, who suggests that "the public worship of the mission community always leads to the pivotal act of sending."[3] Van Gelder also seems to emphasize the "Inside & Out" role of worship when he claims, "The Sunday morning service is the place where the people who worship God become equipped and prepared to do the work of mission that extends that worship into the world."[4]

However, with a few exceptions, it appears that most missional advocates would consider the "Inside Out" view to be the best expression of the primary relationship between worship and mission. They understand worship to be primarily about believers worshiping God, but they see this event as necessarily public and evangelistically potent, and therefore they are concerned that the worship service be accessible and intelligible to believers and unbelievers alike. For example, Guder specifically emphasizes the "public" nature of corporate worship[5] and thus argues that "the language we use, the forms of communication we adopt, the music and symbolism, the liturgies—all of this can and must be translated for the sake of the witness we are to be and do."[6] Stetzer is even more adamant about this point when he insists that "the church and its worship are not intended solely for believers,"[7] and thus "one of the most effective evangelistic methods a church can use is

---

2. Thomas H. Schattauer, *Inside Out: Worship in an Age of Mission* (Minneapolis: Fortress Press, 1999), 2–3.

3. Guder, *Missional Church*, 243.

4. Van Gelder, *The Missional Church and Leadership Formation*, 101.

5. Guder, *Missional Church*, 242.

6. Guder, *The Continuing Conversion of the Church*, 96.

7. Stetzer, *Planting Missional Churches*, 260.

exposing the unchurched to the authentic worship of God."[8] But like Guder, Stetzer insists that one of the necessary components of this evangelistic worship is that the elements of worship be comprehensible to unbelievers. He explains, "My main concern is that the actions of the church are understandable to the unchurched, sensitive to their needs, but not changing the message to be sensitive."[9] Driscoll as well stresses the need to "make the church culturally accessible,"[10] and Tim Keller insists that a church must "adapt its worship because of the presence of unbelievers."[11]

So how can the worship service itself be evangelistic? Although Sally Morgenthaler disagrees with the notion that worship serves mission, she does offer two ways in which worship can be evangelistic.[12] First, the content of the worship elements itself reveals God to the unbelievers. Second, unbelievers will witness the relationship between God and the worshipers and thus be drawn to him. Other missional writers reflect this two-fold evangelistic power of worship as well. Guder's "four basic affirmations" about the purpose of worship resemble this, in which he emphasizes that "worship is the public celebration of the presence and reality of God," that it is a means to "acknowledge, praise, and thank God," and that worship reveals a relationship between God and believers by offering "assurance, comfort, and encouragement."[13] One of his affirmations, however, reveals a third way worship can be evangelistic, and that is in how the gospel itself is proclaimed through "Word and Sacrament and our response to it."[14] Stetzer demonstrates a combination of these purposes when he argues that "the purpose of worship is also to allow unbelievers to observe the divine-human encounter and to yearn for their own personal relationship with God."[15]

Therefore, according to missional authors, worship can accomplish mission in three different ways: (1) by revealing God, (2) by manifesting the relationship between believers and God, and (3) by proclaiming the gospel through the liturgy itself.

---

8. Ibid., 263.
9. Ibid.
10. Driscoll and Breshears, *Vintage Church*, 289.
11. Timothy J. Keller, "Evangelistic Worship," June 2001, http://download.redeemer.com/pdf/learn/resources/Evangelistic_Worship-Keller.pdf.
12. Sally Morgenthaler, *Worship Evangelism: Inviting Unbelievers into the Presence of God* (Grand Rapids: Zondervan, 1999), 88.
13. Guder, *Missional Church*, 242.
14. Ibid.
15. Stetzer, *Planting Missional Churches*, 261.

Twenty-first Century Western Postmodernism as Missional Worship Context.

According to missional authors, the Christendom model significantly affects how the average twenty-first-century American church practices worship. During the Christendom period, the church dominated the culture, and therefore the forms used in worship were in many ways indistinguishable from the forms of Western culture. According to Murray, Sunday as a holy day, the clergy/laity distinction, and even the idea of church buildings all stem from a Christendom model rather than from the New Testament.[16] Roxburgh argues that Christendom had a profound effect on corporate worship. He suggests that worship after Constantine was considerably shaped by "empire and basilica," not Scripture. The Reformation changed things only to make worship more pedagogical, and post-Enlightenment worship became more professional.[17]

Missional advocates do not see this connection between worship practices and western culture as a good development but rather as something from which churches must break free if they are to reach their culture for the gospel. Mead argues that the "relics" of the Christendom model "hold us hostage to the past and make it difficult to create a new paradigm that can be as compelling for the next age as the Christendom Paradigm has been for the past."[18] With the secularization of the West, the inner culture of the church and that of mainstream civilization have parted, leaving the church and its ancient forms "irrelevant."

The Incarnational Mode of Missional Worship

With regard to the missional movement's understanding of Christendom, it is important to recognize that its leaders saw what happened during this period as little more than the church contextualizing worship to the dominant culture of the civilization. Since Christianity happened to be the foremost religion of the western world, the church was able to reflect easily the culture around it, and thus "attractional" evangelism thrived. But because the West has now moved beyond the Christendom

---

16. See Stuart Murray, *Post-Christendom: Church and Mission in a Strange New World* (Carlisle: Paternoster, 2004), 76–78.
17. Alan J. Roxburgh, "Missional Leadership: Equipping God's People for Mission," in *Missional Church: A Vision for the Sending of the Church in North America,* ed. Darrell Guder (Grand Rapids: Wm. B. Eerdmans, 1998), 192–94.
18. Mead, *The Once and Future Church,* 18.

era, missional writers insist that the church must once again learn how to contextualize worship to the dominant culture since one of the key values of the missional movement is incarnation.

For the missional church, worship expressions must reflect the dominant cultural forms of the target group. Guder argues that worship services "must be substantially changed in many settings in our world."[19] Stetzer likewise insists that "worship must take on the expression that reflects the culture of the worshiper if it is to be authentic and make an impact."[20] He sees this contextualization as a self-evident reality in which all churches take part when they use the common language of the people to whom they minister. Specifically addressing musical styles, Stetzer suggests that a church should seek to discover what styles are dominant in its target "focus group" and "adapt [its] own tunes and styles to the preferred styles of [its] focus group."[21]

Contextualization is a significant emphasis of Hirsch, who argues that "worship style, social dynamics, [and] liturgical expressions must result from the process of contextualizing the gospel in any given culture."[22] Driscoll based his entire church planting strategy on the principle of contextualization, arguing that churches must be willing to change regularly their worship forms "in an effort to effectively communicate the gospel to as many people as possible in the cultures around them."[23] Likewise, according to Lepinski, "The need for the Church to remain effective in speaking the 'current language' and to successfully engage all people and age groups is a practice that can be seen in the life of Jesus. Christ's earthly life manifests the importance of relevancy."[24]

For all practical purposes, this implies a view of cultural neutrality, at least in the forms themselves if not always the content. Several authors mention that Christians will need to reject some elements of culture, but usually this refers to the subject matter of songs or movies, for example, rather than the cultural forms themselves. Various content may

19. Guder, *The Continuing Conversion of the Church*, 96.
20. Stetzer and Putman, *Breaking the Missional Code*, 100.
21. Ibid., 64.
22. Hirsch, *The Forgotten Ways*, 143.
23. Driscoll, *Radical Reformission*, 80.
24. Jon Paul Lepinski, "Engaging Postmoderns in Worship: A Study of Effective Techniques and Methods Utilized by Two Growing Churches in Northern California" (D.Min. thesis, Liberty Theological Seminary, 2010), 6.

be immoral, but the culture itself is neutral. This is no more evident than when missional writers discuss music in worship. Guder insists that music must be "translated for the sake of the witness we are to be and do" and says nothing about the possibility that certain styles might be unusable.[25] Stetzer specifically states that "there is no such thing as Christian music, only Christian lyrics"[26] and that "God has no preference regarding style,"[27] implying that cultural forms are neutral and only lyrics may be judged as moral or immoral. Driscoll implies the neutrality of culture by insisting that "it was God who created cultures,"[28] thereby rendering various cultural forms intrinsically good. Parris gets to the root of the issue by insisting that since "a single biblical style is not commanded in Scripture,"[29] cultural styles are neutral. Since culture is inherently neutral according to missional advocates, contextualization becomes as simple as discovering the dominant cultural forms of a target group and reflecting them in worship.

In missional thinking, two important reasons necessitate that worship must be contextualized. The first is that worship must be intelligible to unbelievers, which has already been discussed above. But the second reason worship must be contextualized is that even believers have been shaped by the dominant culture, and so for worship to be intelligible and even authentic for them, the forms used in worship should reflect the outside culture. Guder exemplifies this thinking when he argues, "Our changing cultural context also requires that we change our worship forms so that Christians shaped by late modernity can express their faith authentically and honestly."[30] Driscoll also implies this when he notes that "God promised that people from every race, culture, language, and nation will be present to worship him as their culture follows them into heaven,"[31] which follows the same line of reasoning as Hirsch when he claims that "it is from within their own cultural expressions that the nations will

---

25. Guder, *The Continuing Conversion of the Church*, 96.
26. Stetzer, *Planting Missional Churches*, 267.
27. Elmer Towns and Edward Stetzer, *Perimeters of Light: Biblical Boundaries for the Emerging Church* (Chicago: Moody Publishers, 2004), 43.
28. Driscoll, *Radical Reformission*, 80.
29. Parris, "Instituting a Missional Worship Style," 2.
30. Guder, *The Continuing Conversion of the Church*, 157.
31. Driscoll, *Radical Reformission*, 100.

worship."[32] This reasoning is primary in Kimball's thinking, who argues that "since worship is about our expressing love and adoration to God, and leaders teaching people about God, then of course the culture will shape our expressions of worship."[33]

Preliminary Evaluation

There is little doubt that the missional church movement has been influential in evangelical churches and that it continues to grow. Having surveyed the history and theology of this important movement and specifically its impact upon the worship of evangelical churches, the question remains as to whether this influence has been beneficial or not. This concluding section offers some suggestions of positive contributions missional thinking has made to evangelical worship as well as a few areas that will require further critical evaluation in the rest of the book.

Positive

I believe the missional church movement has provided positive change in at least three important areas of thinking.

Focus on Evangelism. First, the missional church movement's strong emphasis upon every Christian participating in fervent evangelism is quite welcome. Whether or not one agrees with the *missio Dei* emphasis of the missional church movement, its focus on evangelism that is profoundly God-centered and more than an invitation to come to a seeker service is a refreshing development in how evangelical churches understand missions.

Recovery of Believer's Worship. This refocus on the proper place of evangelism has led to another beneficial contribution—the recovery of worship as primarily a believers' service to God rather than a "seeker" event. Regardless of the various degrees of connection between worship and evangelism that missional writers advocate, each of them insists upon worship that consists primarily of believers directing their attention toward God in a meaningful way. This has led to several side benefits, such

---

32. Hirsch, *The Forgotten Ways*, 138.
33. Kimball, *Emerging Worship*, 2009 298.

as a recovery of congregational singing with more substantive content rather than performance in worship to attract seekers. Additionally, the missional emphasis of true worship itself having evangelistic benefit seems to fit biblical teaching (e.g. 1 Cor. 14:23–25) better than the seeker model.

Recognition of Changes in Western Culture. The missional movement has also done evangelical churches a service by articulating the nature of the Christendom model of western culture and identifying the significant shifts that took place in the West post-Enlightenment. In particular, missional authors' explanations of how the Enlightenment and modernist thinking has shaped evangelical churches in the West are a necessary tool for the evaluation of church practice and worship today.

Points for Evaluation
At least three key areas of thought in missional thinking, however, require critical evaluation.

Interpretation of Christendom. First, although the missional church seems to correctly recognize the nature of the Christendom paradigm in western civilization and in many cases rightly discerns the integral relationship between Christianity and culture during that period, it appears to view this development in the history of the church as entirely negative, with very few positive fruits. At the very least, most missional advocates see what happened as merely neutral contextualization of the church's worship to culture, yet their very quick dismissal of worship forms coming out of that period as simply antiquated "relics" reveals what may be a simplistic understanding of the impact of the church upon culture during that period. This perspective limits their ability to recognize the strengths of the cultural forms from that period in expressing Christian values and the vast differences that exist today with regard to culture and contextualization in worship.

Understanding of Culture. Yet perhaps this first criticism is merely a symptom of a greater problem, and that is a fundamental misunderstanding of the nature of culture. Most missional authors assume the neutrality of culture itself as self-evident, never seeking to prove such a point beyond shallow arguments such as comparing the accommodation of cultural forms to the adoption of common languages or insisting that the Bible does not prescribe particular forms. Missional authors have failed to engage serious thinking on the matter of culture that suggests an inseparable connection between religion, beliefs, values, worldviews, and cultural expressions. They devote much too little space to consideration of how the modern idea of culture relates to the biblical realities of "the world," human depravity, admonitions to be holy, and the ever-present danger of religious syncretism.

Understanding of Worship. Finally, how the missional church views the nature of worship itself requires more careful evaluation. Beyond brief mention of a few proof texts that seem to indicate a connection between worship and evangelism, missional authors have failed to wrestle with this relationship at a significant level, and instead find themselves closely resembling the "attractional" church growth models they repudiate. In fact, Sally Morgenthaler, whose purpose in writing *Worship Evangelism* was to discourage such models in favor of active daily evangelism on the part of every believer, later discovered that her book instead served to fuel the attractional model.[34] Missional thinkers need to give more serious consideration to the effects that focusing heavily on evangelism in worship have upon the quality of the worship itself.

The missional church movement has had significant impact upon worship in evangelical churches. It has caused churches to give much more careful consideration to how much of their worship methodology has been shaped by culture rather than Scripture and how they can recover believers' worship that had been lost in many churches' evangelistic restructuring, while nevertheless making worship intelligible to unbelievers.

Yet in its noble ambition to recover truly missional worship, the missional church movement may have failed to recognize how its own understanding of both worship and culture has been shaped by the Christendom and Enlightenment models it condemns. Therefore, the full correction of errors regarding worship and evangelism that missional advocates rightly identify requires more careful study of culture and worship and their relation to evangelism from a biblical perspective.

---

34. Sally Morgenthaler, "Worship as Evangelism," *Rev! Magazine*, June 2007.

The Strange Land

Essential to the missional church movement's philosophy of evangelism and worship is their understanding of culture. Since they articulate incarnation and contextualization as important postures for accomplishing the *missio Dei*, missional proponents consistently discuss the importance of understanding culture, reaching culture, engaging culture, and redeeming culture. Therefore, an investigation into what they commonly mean by "culture" is necessary in order to more thoroughly evaluate their incarnational philosophy. I will synthesize the missional understanding of culture and contextualization here, revealing influences leading to this thinking.

Common Missional Definitions of Culture

Likely the most influential early evangelical definition of culture comes from Lesslie Newbigin, who claims that culture is "the sum total of ways of living built up by a human community and transmitted from one generation to another."[35] Darrell Guder cites this definition early in *Missional Church*,[36] thus revealing its impact upon later missional thinking in the Gospel and Our Culture Network and beyond. Other later definitions reflect similar thinking. For example, Alan and Debra Hirsch maintain, "Culture is a complex jungle of ideas, history, language, religious views, economic systems, political issues, and the like."[37] Kathy Black defines culture as "the sum attitudes, customs, and beliefs that distinguishes one group of people from another. Culture is transmitted through language, material objects, ritual, institutions, and art forms from one generation to the next."[38]

Important to recognize is that none of these definitions draws its understanding of culture directly from Scripture but rather assumes the validity of the contemporary idea of culture on its own merits. Furthermore, beyond these few definitions, other missional authors seem to assume the idea of culture without even defining it, revealing that they utilize the

---

35. Newbigin, *The Other Side of 1984*, 5.
36. Guder, *Missional Church*, 9.
37. Alan Hirsch and Debra Hirsch, *Untamed: Reactivating a Missional Form of Discipleship* (Grand Rapids: Baker Books, 2010), 25.
38. Kathy Black, *Culturally-Conscious Worship* (St. Louis: Chalice Press, 2000), 8.

prevailing contemporary notion of culture by default in their emphases upon incarnation and contextualization. This in itself is not necessarily problematic, but in order to understand what missional proponents mean by "culture," this requires further research into what led to the development of the idea as it exists today.

The Historical Development of the Missional Idea of Culture

Historically, the term "culture" did not emerge in its common use until the late eighteenth century. The term itself is much older, its Latin roots planted squarely in discussion of agriculture. As early as 1776, however, the term began to be used metaphorically to describe what Matthew Arnold would later call "the best which has been thought and said in the world."[39] The term used this way first entered German philosophy in Johann Gottfried Herder's *Reflections on the Philosophy of History* (1776), in which he argued that each civilization progresses through a process of enlightenment at which point it begins to produce "culture." Thus the term was first used to describe what would today be more commonly called "high culture" or "the arts." This introduced a new vocabulary for describing differences among people groups, but it was not until the rise of the formal discipline of cultural anthropology that the broader idea of culture took its present form.

Darwinian evolutionism influenced all aspects of human inquiry in the mid-nineteenth century, including explanation of cultural differences. For example, Edward Tylor, the founding father of British anthropology, developed a theory of cultural evolution that describes stages of human history from primitivism to advancement. Tylor's attempt to explain differences among various people groups led to the formation of the discipline of cultural anthropology. This new discipline involved "the description, interpretation, and analysis of similarities and differences in human cultures."[40] Tylor's ideas reflect Herder's, but his understanding of culture was much broader. Instead of defining culture as the more advanced achievements of a society, Tylor defined it as "that complex whole which includes knowledge, belief, art, morals, law, custom, and any other capa-

---

39. Matthew Arnold, *Culture and Anarchy: An Essay in Political and Social Criticism* (London: Smith, Elder, and Co, 1869), viii.
40. Jenell Williams Paris and Brian M. Howell, *Introducing Cultural Anthropology: A Christian Perspective* (Grand Rapids: Baker Academic, 2010), 4.

bilities and habits acquired by man as a member of society."[41] Important to this definition is that everything in human society is a subset of the broader idea of culture, even religion; the subtitle to Tylor's monumental book reveals different aspects of what he understood as culture: "Mythology, Philosophy, Religion, Art, and Custom." Schusky explains how this all-encompassing definition of culture developed to form the field of anthropology:

> Scholars recast the history of marriage, religion, politics, the family, mythology, and other social forms, speculating on their origin and stage of evolution. Because such a wide variety of forms were examined, some intellectuals concluded that all aspects of human behavior were valid fields for study. Organization of the study should fall to anthropology, and its concept of culture should be such as to allow investigation of all these facets of human activity.[42]

Tylor was also an early advocate of cultural relativism, "the judgment of a practice only in relation to its cultural setting."[43]

The anthropological notion of culture took a third step in America with Franz Boas, whom Jerry Moore calls "the most important single force in shaping American anthropology."[44] Boas shifted cultural anthropology from an evolutionist position to what is called Historicism, which argues that cultures are not progressive advancements of one continuous evolutionary development, but rather each distinct culture is a product of very specific historical contexts and thus can be understood only in light of those contexts. He argued, "in place of a single line of evolution there appears a multiplicity of converging and diverging lines which it is difficult to bring under one system."[45] He was

41. Edward B. Tylor, *Primitive Culture: Researches into the Development of Mythology, Philosophy, Religion, Art, and Custom* (London: John Murray, 1871), 1.
42. Ernest Lester Schusky, *The Study of Cultural Anthropology* (New York: Holt, Rinehart and Winston, 1975), 10.
43. Ibid., 15.
44. Jerry D. Moore, *Visions of Culture: An Introduction to Anthropological Theories and Theorists* (Lanham, MD: Rowman Altamira, 2009), 42.
45. Franz Boas, "The History of Anthropology," in *A Franz Boas Reader: The Shaping of American Anthropology, 1883-1911*, ed. George W. Stocking, Jr. (Chicago: The University of Chicago Press, 1989), 34.

among the first to speak of plural cultures that share no direct connections; similarities that exist between cultures, Boas argued, are purely arbitrary or at most due to similar historical situations, an idea called Particularism. This further reinforced the notion of cultural relativism, denying any universal laws of culture and advancing the idea that cultures with different historical backgrounds may not be compared at all. Every cultural expression is learned within a particular historical setting; nothing is innate. This view of human culture became widely established, especially in American anthropology, becoming the *de facto* explanation for differences among civilizations.[46]

The missional idea of culture, then, took shape within this anthropological climate. Charles H. Kraft acknowledges that the missional idea of culture draws from cultural anthropology: "When it comes to the analysis of such cultural contexts, however, it is likely that contemporary disciplines such as anthropology and linguistics, dedicated as they are to a primary focus on these issues, may be able to provide us with sharper tools for analysis than the disciplines of history and philology have provided."[47] Even if not deliberately, however, most missional authors adapt the view of culture held by cultural anthropologists. For example, one cannot help but notice the similarity between Tylor's influential definition of culture ("that complex whole which includes knowledge, belief, art, morals, law, custom, and any other capabilities and habits acquired by man as a member of society"[48]) and Newbigin's definition ("the sum total of ways of living built up by a human community and transmitted from one generation to another"[49]). Yet the connection runs deeper than similarities between definitions. Like cultural anthropology, the missional church views the idea of culture and particular cultural expressions as neutral. Cultures develop independently of each other and may not be compared. Evangelical authors may cite specific content as sinful, but no cultural expression is unredeemable. Mark Snoeberger helpfully summarizes a common evangelical view of cultural neutrality:

---

46. George W. Stocking, Jr., "Franz Boas and the Culture Concept in Historical Perspective," *American Anthropologist* 68 (1966): 867–82.
47. Charles H. Kraft, "Interpreting in Cultural Context," *Journal of the Evangelical Theological Society* 21, no. 4 (December 1978): 358.
48. Tylor, *Primitive Culture*, 1.
49. Newbigin, *The Other Side of 1984*, 5.

> There is a general assumption that culture is neutral, and either independent of or essentially in harmony with God: just as man retains the image of God in microcosm, so culture retains the image of God in macrocosm. As such, culture possesses aspects and attributes that escape, to a large extent, the effects of depravity. The Christian response to culture is merely to bridle various aspects of culture and employ them for their divinely intended end—glory of God.[50]

Most importantly, like cultural anthropologists, missional advocates understand religion as but one component of culture rather than the other way around. For example, the Hirsches list "religious views" as one element of culture,[51] and Newbigin himself states unequivocally, "Religion—including the Christian religion—is thus part of culture."[52] This position is also clear in their discussion of the relationship between culture and evangelism. According to missional authors, the gospel must be "contextualized" in a given culture so that the recipients will accept the message and change their religion, but the culture itself must not change. John Stott insists that conversion will not mean a change of culture: "True, conversion involves repentance, and repentance is renunciation. Yet this does not require the convert to step right out of his former culture into a Christian subculture which is totally distinctive."[53] Additionally, Driscoll explains that the gospel "must be fitted to" culture.[54] New believers are thus encouraged to worship using the cultural forms most natural to them. Religion changes while culture remains unchanged, signifying that religion is only one element within the larger idea of culture.

This idea of culture is an essential component of the missional approach to all aspects of church ministry, including evangelism and worship. The modern definition of culture developed out of relatively recent ideas about anthropology. Prior to the Enlightenment, people groups were differentiated primarily by their religion; later, the way to account

---

50. Mark A. Snoeberger, "Noetic Sin, Neutrality, and Contextualization: How Culture Receives the Gospel," *Detroit Baptist Seminary Journal* 9 (2004): 357.
51. Hirsch and Hirsch, *Untamed*, 25.
52. Newbigin, *The Other Side of 1984*, 5.
53. Stott, *Christian Mission in the Modern World*, 181.
54. Driscoll, *Radical Reformission*, 20.

for differences was "culture." Neither New Testament authors nor pre-Enlightenment Christian authors discuss "culture" as such.

However, the fact that the contemporary idea of culture emerged from twentieth-century cultural anthropology does not necessarily imply that it is an invalid or unbiblical idea. Many traditional ideas take on contemporary articulations. The important question for a biblical evaluation of the common missional understanding of culture is to evaluate how their approach to this subject fits within a biblical framework. It is to that topic I turn next.

chapter 4

SINGING THE SONGS OF BABYLON:

A HISTORY OF CONTEXTUALIZATION

And the herald proclaimed aloud,
"You are commanded, O peoples, nations, and languages,
that when you hear the sound of the horn, pipe, lyre, trigon,
harp, bagpipe, and every kind of music,
you are to fall down and worship the golden image
that King Nebuchadnezzar has set up."
Daniel 3:4–5

The music played, and Shadrach, Meshach, and Abednego refused to worship. The story of the fiery furnace is a familiar one, but we often forget about the numerous other Hebrews who were also captives in that strange land and present at the dedication of Nebuchadnezzar's image. Apparently they not only joined with the songs of Babylon, they also bowed to the image of its king!

Conflicting Christian approaches to culture is not a new phenomenon. The Hebrews themselves struggled with the issue even though as a theocracy, religion and culture were theoretically inseparable in the nation of Israel. Even so, more often than not the Hebrews failed to relate biblically to the nations around them, and their perpetual syncretism led to their eventual demise.

With the birth of the church, however, biblical religion and national identity became distinct, and thus the struggle of how to relate to culture entered a new and perhaps more difficult phase. The story of this struggle provides the historical material in which different Christian approaches to culture find their justification. Thus a brief survey of this struggle will set a discussion of these approaches in their proper historical context.

Essentially, the missional emphasis of contextualization is a natural application of the newly developed anthropological view of culture. Out of a desire to reach a culture with the gospel, many evangelicals believe that the message must be adjusted to cultural contexts.

Yet this missional desire to contextualize the gospel message sits within a tension that exists for Christians seeking to follow the Lord's claim that they are in the world but not of the world (John 17:6–19), well-illustrated in the immortal words from the pen of early church father Tertullian of Carthage, "What indeed has Athens to do with Jerusalem?"[1] Missional church advocates in particular, with their strong emphasis on cultural incarnation, have once again raised this perennial question: How should Christians respond to the cultures of unbelievers around them?

For centuries tension between the biblical realities of God's good creation and the world's corruption have caused Christians to debate the proper Christian approach to culture. Michael Horton summarizes well the conflict between approaches to culture:

> It was confusing to grow up singing both "This World Is Not My Home" and "This Is My Father's World." Those hymns embody two common and seemingly contradictory Christian responses to culture. One sees this world as a wasteland of godlessness, with which the Christian should have as little as possible to do. The other regards cultural transformation as virtually identical to "kingdom activity."[2]

This conflict, combined with the biblical mandate to reach the world, creates the missional dilemma. Missional church advocates have tended to

---

1. Tertullian, *The Prescription against Heretics*, vol. 3, Ante-Nicene Fathers (Grand Rapids: Wm. B. Eerdmans, 1951), 246.
2. Michael S. Horton, "How the Kingdom Comes," *Christianity Today* 50, no. 1 (January 2006): 42–46.

stress creation's goodness and the need to contextualize the gospel in order to reach the culture. Yet their answer to this age-old question is not novel; rather, it fits well within a standard, historical approach to culture. This chapter will explore the roots of the idea of contextualization, survey typical approaches, and identify where the missional posture fits in the history.

Roots of Contextualization

The missional adaptation of the anthropological definition of culture provides the foundation for the missional objective of contextualization. Like the idea of culture, the term "contextualization" is a relatively recent development. Hesselgrave and Rommen provide a helpful survey of contextualization's history in *Contextualization: Meanings, Methods, and Models*.[3] The idea of contextualization is rooted in the missions debates of the Division on World Missions and Evangelism (DWME) of the World Council of Churches (WCC). Influenced by the anthropological understanding of culture and thus concerned that each civilization develop its own theology and method of church ministry in its own cultural context, the DWME began to condemn the "theological imperialism" of the church in the West. Its 1972–73 Bangkok Conference argued that non-Western churches should develop their own ideas "in a theology, a liturgy, a praxis, a form of community, rooted in their own culture."[4] This desire for each church to be indigenized within its culture, clearly influenced by a Historicism view of culture and a belief in cultural neutrality, became known as "contextualization." Hesselgrave and Rommen explain how this new concept differed from previous ways of thinking:

> Contextualization is a new word—a technical neologism. It may also signal a new (or renewed) sensitivity to the need for adaptation to cultural context. To its originators it involved a new point of departure and a new approach to theologizing and to theological education: namely, praxis or involvement in the struggle for justice within the existential situation in which men and women

3. David J. Hesselgrave and Edward Rommen, *Contextualization: Meanings, Methods, and Models* (Pasadena, CA: William Carey Library, 2003), 28–35.
4. "Your Kingdom Come" (a pamphlet published by the World Conference on Mission and Evangelism, n.d.), 5.

find themselves today. As such it goes well beyond the concept of indigenization which Henry Venn, Rufus Anderson, and their successors defined in terms of an autonomous (self-supporting, self-governing, and self-propagating) church.[5]

Byang H. Kato explains the importance of this development:

> This is a new term imported into theology to express a deeper concept than indigenization ever does. We understand the term to mean making concepts or ideals relevant in a given situation. In reference to Christian practices, it is an effort to express the never changing Word of God in ever changing modes of relevance. Since the Gospel message is inspired but the mode of its expression is not, contextualization of the modes of expression is not only right but necessary.[6]

Like many of the missiological ideas that sprang from the WCC discussions of the 1970s, the idea of contextualization originally implied a relativism in every aspect of the church, including potentially theology and even morality. Conservative evangelicals adopted the term but reshaped it to mean communication of an unchanging biblical message in changing cultural expressions. Hesselgrave and Rommen explain:

> Most conservative evangelicals were already enamored with the word *contextualization*. They chose to adopt and redefine it where they rejected the meaning prescribed by the TEF [Theological Education Fund] initiators. They agreed that the new definition should reveal a sensitivity to context and a fidelity to Scripture.[7]

They go on to explain how these conservative evangelicals disagreed on particular nuances of their new definition and note that "there is not yet a commonly accepted definition of the word *contextualization*."[8]

---

5. Hesselgrave and Rommen, *Contextualization*, 32.
6. Byang H. Kato, "The Gospel, Cultural Context and Religious Syncretism," in *Let the Earth Hear His Voice*, ed. J. D. Douglas (Minneapolis: World Wide Publications, 1975), 1217.
7. Hesselgrave and Rommen, *Contextualization*, 33. Emphasis original.
8. Ibid., 35. Emphasis original.

Part of Hesselgrave and Rommen's motive for writing their book is to offer some clarity on this problem, and their conclusions strongly influenced the contemporary missional understanding of contextualization. In particular, Hesselgrave and Rommen distinguish between cultural contextualization and theological contextualization, and they insist that biblical contextualization must be "true to both indigenous culture and the authority of Scripture."[9] In other words, a conservative evangelical will not change the essential message of the gospel, but everything else is merely "cultural" and must be contextualized. Thus Hesselgrave and Rommen's definition of contextualization has been adopted to a significant extent by missional advocates:

> Christian contextualization can be thought of as the attempt to communicate the message of the person, works, Word, and will of God in a way that is faithful to God's revelation, especially as it is put forth in the teachings of Holy Scripture, and that is meaningful to respondents in their respective cultural and existential contexts. Contextualization is both verbal and non-verbal and has to do with theologizing; Bible translation, interpretation, and application; incarnational lifestyle; evangelism; Christian instruction; church planting and growth; church organization; worship style—indeed all of those activities involved in carrying out the Great Commission.[10]

Christ and Culture

Likely one of the most influential works to articulate the different Christian approaches to culture is H. Richard Niebuhr's monumental *Christ and Culture*.[11] Niebuhr names five "ideal types" that have become standard in such discussions: Christ against culture, the Christ of culture, Christ above culture, Christ and culture in paradox, and Christ the transformer of culture. His second type is outside the bounds of this paper since it essentially assumes that Christianity itself is merely a product of

---

9. Ibid., 55.
10. Ibid., 200.
11. H. Richard Niebuhr, *Christ and Culture* (Harper & Row, 1975).

culture and has no Scriptural foundation.[12] This leaves four evangelical types, which summarize the general positions to be explored in this section. Christ against culture represents the most extreme position and will characterize the radical reformers and their descendants. The opposite extreme is Christ above culture, which is essentially the Christendom position detailed below. In the middle are the two predominant views that have come to characterize post-Christendom Protestantism: Christ and culture in paradox and Christ the transformer of culture. In the former category, what has come to be generally called the two-kingdom doctrine, Niebuhr lists Martin Luther as an early proponent; in the latter, a position known more commonly as the transformationalist view, he includes Augustine and John Calvin as advocates. As the discussion below will reveal, these categorizations are often debated, yet the types do provide helpful descriptions of what occurred historically. Post-Christendom evangelical approaches to culture are largely a debate between the two-kingdom advocates and the transformationalists.

Historic Approaches to Culture

Christendom

Before exploring approaches to cultural engagement post-Christendom, or even that of Christendom itself, it is necessary to consider what happened before and immediately after the Edict of Milan in 313. Early debates about approaches to culture are evident, for example, in differences between Tertullian (c. 160–c. 225), quoted above for his emphasis on the antithesis between Christianity and pagan philosophy, and his contemporary, Clement of Alexandria (c. 150–c. 215), who interacted positively with Greek philosophy in his Christian polemics.[13] Thus the tension between antithesis and commonality begins quite early. How-

---

12. Carson makes this point: "In Niebuhr's analysis, Gnosticism and liberalism constitute the major proponents of the second of his five patterns, namely, 'the Christ of culture.' If sober reflection commends the conclusions that neither is a Christian movement in any sense worthy of the adjective 'Christian,' then not much is left of this second category. . . . In this endeavor to ground his patterns in the Bible, he is less than successful with the second: the 'Christ of culture' pattern pays scant attention to Scripture and then leaps to the two dominant movements, Gnosticism and liberalism, that are themselves least grounded in Scripture" (D. A. Carson, *Christ and Culture Revisited* [Grand Rapids: Wm. B. Eerdmans, 2008], 36).

13. M. L. W. Laistner, *Christianity and Pagan Culture in the Later Roman Empire* (Ithaca, NY: Cornell University Press, 1979), 58–59.

ever, even those like Clement who were willing to engage with pagan thought on its own terms were not tolerant of every aspect of pagan society; indeed, while Clement appreciated some aspects of Greek philosophy, he repudiated Gnosticism and spoke out against pagan music.[14] This kind of critical eye toward all aspects of pagan culture characterizes many of these early theologians, especially with regard to cultural practices that came directly from pagan practices, music in particular. James McKinnon suggests that "there is hardly a major church father from the fourth century who does not inveigh against pagan musical practice in the strongest language,"[15] and Calvin Stapert notes that this

> uniformity is especially striking considering how different those writers were in other respects. Whether they were Greek-speaking or Latin-speaking, pre- or post-Constantine, conciliatory or antagonistic toward pagan learning, lifelong Christians or converts—whatever their background or personality, they agreed that Christians should distance themselves from some of the music of the surrounding culture.[16]

These sorts of tensions are evident in early Christian documents such as the first-century *Didache* and especially in the anonymous second-century *Epistle to Diognetus*. The *Didache* emphasizes the antithesis that exists between the "two ways, one of life and one of death; and between the two ways there is a great difference."[17] The *Epistle to Diognetus* affirms this antithesis as well, but goes one step further by suggesting that there also exists commonality between the two, again presenting a tension between being in, but not of, the world.

The legalization of Christianity by Emperor Constantine in 313 and establishment of Christianity as the official religion of the empire in 380

---

14. Clement of Alexandria, *The Instructor*, vol. 2, Ante-Nicene Fathers (Grand Rapids: Wm. B. Eerdmans, 1986), 248–49; Clement of Alexandria, *Miscellanies*, vol. 2, Ante-Nicene Fathers (Grand Rapids: Wm. B. Eerdmans, 1986), 500–501.

15. James W. McKinnon, *Music in Early Christian Literature* (Cambridge: Cambridge University Press, 1989), 2.

16. Calvin R. Stapert, *A New Song for an Old World: Musical Thought in the Early Church* (Grand Rapids: Wm. B. Eerdmans, 2006), 131.

17. Cyril C. Richardson, ed., "The Teaching of the Twelve Apostles, Commonly Called the Didache," in *Early Christian Fathers* (New York: Collier, 1970), 171.

change the situation somewhat. Some, such as Eusebius (263–339), argue that the Roman Empire is now allied to the church, and the full "Christianization" of society is now underway.[18] Eusebius's idea of one-kingdom is eventually adopted by the church during the medieval period, creating what is today known as "Christendom"—an essential fusion of church and state during this time.

The position of Augustine (354–430) in this discussion is highly debated. Some, such as Niebuhr, place him in the transformationalist camp. Others, such as David VanDrunen, insist that Augustine once again articulates the tension between antithesis and commonality first expressed in the *Epistle to Diognetus*.[19] In his monumental *City of God*, Augustine argues that there exists a fundamental hostility between the City of God and the City of Man: "Two cities have been formed by two loves: the earthly by the love of self, even to the contempt of God; the heavenly by the love of God, even to the contempt of self."[20] For Augustine, the City of God exists in heaven, but even now believers constitute the City of God, though currently only as strangers and pilgrims. The City of Man consists of all unbelievers, and thus these two cities will perpetuate into eternity. Augustine understands these cities to be two completely separate identities distinguished by different lifestyles and loves; however, since the two cities are now "commingled, and as it were entangled together,"[21] believers may participate in the City of Man on political and civic levels for the sake of peace. Thus both the themes of antithesis, emphasized in the *Didache*, and commonality, found in the *Epistle to Diognetus*, find expression in Augustine's *City of God*. In many ways, because of his emphasis both on antithesis and commonality, Augustine serves as the fountainhead of both two-kingdom and transformationalist points of view. However, as mentioned earlier, Eusebius's argument eventually takes hold and becomes the Christ above culture framework for the rest of Christendom, especially after Emperor Theodosius I declared all paganism illegal in 395.

---

18. Eusebius, *Ecclesiastical History*, trans. Roy J. Deferrari, vol. 29, The Fathers of the Church (New York: Fathers of the Church, 1955), 10.1, 3–4, 8–9.
19. David VanDrunen, *Natural Law and the Two Kingdoms: A Study in the Development of Reformed Social Thought* (Grand Rapids: Wm. B. Eerdmans, 2009), 26.
20. Augustine, *City of God*, trans. Marcus Dods (New York: The Modern Library, 1950), 28.
21. Ibid., 11.1.

Martin Luther

When Martin Luther (1483–1546) begins making reforms in the church, one of the most significant issues he faces is the relationship between the civil and ecclesiastical authorities. Thus, Luther articulates an understanding of antithesis and commonality that in many ways reflects previous thought but in such a way that he is often credited as the first to express a robust two-kingdom doctrine. Luther, like Augustine before him, articulates a doctrine of two metaphysical kingdoms, one comprised of believers and the other of unbelievers. And, as in the *Epistle to Diognetus* and *City of God*, he argues for a strict antithesis between the two kingdoms:

> There are two kingdoms, one the kingdom of God, the other the kingdom of the world. ... God's kingdom is a kingdom of grace and mercy ... but the kingdom of the world is a kingdom of wrath and severity.[22]

However, he also adds thought different from Augustine in that he draws connections to two institutions as well, governments that God has placed over the two kingdoms: the church for the spiritual kingdom and civic governments for the temporal kingdom.[23] The ecclesiastical realm is ruled by Scripture alone and has responsibility over spiritual matters; the civic governments have jurisdiction over temporal matters and are ruled by natural law.

Luther maintains a careful distinction between kingdoms and their governments, arguing that each government has jurisdiction only in matters given to them; he insists that temporal authority may "extend no further than to life and property and external affairs on earth, for God cannot and will not permit anyone but himself to rule over the soul."[24] However, Luther does associate the visible aspects of the institutional church with the earthly kingdom (since they are temporal after all), and thus he sees those aspects to be under the jurisdiction of the civil powers.

---

22. Martin Luther, "An Open Letter on the Harsh Book against the Peasants," in *Luther's Works*, ed. Robert C. Schultz and Helmut T. Lehman, vol. 46 (Philadelphia: Fortress Press, 1967), 46:69.
23. Martin Luther, "Temporal Authority: To What Extent It Should Be Obeyed," in *Luther's Works*, ed. Walther I. Brandt and Helmut T. Lehmann, vol. 45 (Philadelphia: Muhlenberg, 1962), 45:85–92.
24. Ibid., 45:104–5.

The Radical Reformers

Following Luther's lead, each Protestant group reacted against the Christendom approach to culture in some way. The most radical rejection of the Christ above culture model of the Roman Church was that of the Anabaptists. Niebuhr categorized them as Christ against culture, and in many ways he was right if by that categorization he meant that they abjectly repudiated any attempt to fuse the ecclesiastical and civic realms characteristic of the Christendom model.

The Anabaptists emerged as a small group of dissidents from within the Swiss reformation led by Ulrich Zwingli (1484–1531). Zwingli fostered many significant reformations in areas of justification and the Lord's Table, but his perspective on church/state relationship was essentially the same as the Church of Rome. He sought to establish his reforms on the civil level and enforce them through the state, including one significant area he did not reform, namely, infant baptism. When a group of his followers under the leadership of Conrad Grebel (1498–1526), Felix Manz (1498–1527), and Menno Simons (1496–1561) developed convictions regarding believer's baptism, they demanded, "You have no authority to place the decision in the hands of My Lords [the city council], for the decision is already made; the Spirit of God decides."[25] They believed that the civil government had no right to enforce laws in areas that belonged to the church.

This view, which was very similar to Luther's discussed above, could be characterized as a modified two-kingdom position, as does Perry Bush, who also notes what likely influenced its essential difference:

> Established or state churches, enjoying a cooperative relationship with the reigning government, have often seen these two realms, each with its own limitations, as two equal spheres of God's activity. ... For groups having a more hostile relationship with the state, however, two-kingdom theology was modified to emphasize separation, not church-state cooperation. Not surprisingly, the theology of nonresistance that Anabaptist reformers passed on to their Mennonite descendants stressed the

---

25. Cited in Cornelius J. Dyck, *An Introduction to Mennonite History: A Popular History of the Anabaptists and the Mennonites* (Scottdale, PA: Herald Press, 1981), 29.

latter course. Given that the governments of their day had vili-
fied, hunted, drowned, and burned them at the stake, Anabaptists bequeathed a negative view of the state, a state from which
Christians could expect great evil.[26]

The Anabaptists differed from Luther concerning the individual Christian's relationship to the civic realm. While Luther maintained a distinction between church and state, he nevertheless taught that Christians
were members of both institutions and thus must submit to both in the
matters under their jurisdiction. The Anabaptists disagreed. They agreed
that the state was necessary in an evil world and were even willing to
submit to the government in civic matters,[27] but unlike Luther, they
rejected political involvement, including holding office, taking oaths,
and especially violence, even when the state was simply exercising its
civic responsibility. This sentiment was expressed by Anabaptists in the
1538 Bern Disputation:

> We grant that in the non-Christian world state authorities have
> a legitimate place, to keep order, to punish evil, and to protect
> the good. But we as Christians live according to the Gospel and
> our only authority and Lord is Jesus Christ. Christians conse-
> quently do not use the sword, which is worldly.[28]

Although they recognized the need for the state to govern the affairs of unbelievers, Christians must not involve themselves in such matters.[29] They even
rejected using "worldly" means to protect themselves. Grebel insisted:

> Moreover, the gospel and its adherents are not to be protected
> by the sword, nor are they thus to protect themselves. ... True
> Christian believers are sheep among wolves, sheep for the slaugh-

---

26. Perry Bush, *Two Kingdoms, Two Loyalties: Mennonite Pacifism in Modern America* (Baltimore:
The Johns Hopkins University Press, 1998), 6–7.

27. Franklin H. Littell, *The Anabaptist View of the Church*, 2nd ed., rev. and enl. (Paris, AR: The
Baptist Standard Bearer, 2001), 106.

28. Jan P. Matthijssen, "The Bern Disputation of 1538," *Mennonite Quarterly Review* 22 (January
1948): 32.

29. James C. Juhnke, *A People of Two Kingdoms: The Political Acculturation of the Kansas Mennonites* (Newton, KS: Faith & Life Press, 1975), 10.

ter; they must be baptized in anguish and affliction ... tried with fire and must reach the fatherland of eternal rest, not by killing their body, but by mortifying their spiritual enemies. Neither do they use worldly sword or war, since all killing has ceased with them.[30]

Very simply, Anabaptists believed that the church had entered a period of compromise and even apostasy during the medieval period, and they included the so-called Magisterial Reformers in this group. Furthermore, since they insisted upon the pursuit of personal holiness, they advocated strict separation from the world.

John Calvin

John Calvin's (1509–1564) position regarding the relationship of the church to the surrounding culture is one of intense debate. For example, VanDrunen argues that Calvin essentially agreed with Luther on the two kingdoms and natural law contrary to the Neo-Calvinists, who insist that their transformationalism comes from him. In fact, VanDrunen argues that H. Richard Niebuhr miscategorized Calvin in his influential taxonomy in *Christ and Culture*.[31]

Like Luther, Calvin saw a fundamental antithesis between the kingdom of God and the kingdom of the world while recognizing a commonality in terms of involvement in the institutions governing each realm.[32] In particular, Calvin expresses God's distinctive rule over both kingdoms in terms of the Son's dual mediatorship, e.g., the fact that the Son is both creator and redeemer and that he rules the kingdom of God as redeemer but the kingdom of the world only as creator.[33] The most significant point of disagreement with Luther is that Calvin believed that Christians were actually members of both kingdoms, not just the institutions associated with those kingdoms.

These similarities with Luther lead some like VanDrunen to insist that Calvin advocated the two-kingdom approach, while others in the Re-

---

30. George H. Williams and Angel M. Mergal, eds., *Spiritual and Anabaptist Writers* (Philadelphia: Westminster, 1957), 80.

31. VanDrunen, *Natural Law and the Two Kingdoms*, 69ff.

32. John Calvin, *Institutes of the Christian Religion* (Philadelphia: Westminster John Knox Press, 1960), 3.19.15.

33. Ibid., 1.13.7; 2.12.6.

formed tradition agree with Niebuhr's categorization of Calvin as a trans-formationalist. For example, Jason Lief argues that Calvin's two-kingdom motif differs more significantly than VanDrunen wants to acknowledge and actually affirms later transformationalist models rooted in an escha-tological foundation.[34]

Abraham Kuyper

This history of Christian approaches to culture clearly enters a stage of transition, however, in the work of Dutch Reformed theologian Abraham Kuyper (1837–1920). VanDrunen argues that Kuyper re-tained enough of the important categories of two-kingdom theology to be categorized squarely in its line of thought. In fact, even one-kingdom proponents such as Jeremy Begbie acknowledge this, especially citing the fact that Kuyper grounded culture in the created order rather than in redemption.[35] Others, however, disagree, arguing that Kuyper moved significantly enough away from two-kingdom thinking, especially with his view of natural law. John Frame, for example, calls VanDrunen's claim a "very implausible position."[36]

Despite this debate, Kuyper at the very least serves as a transitional figure between typical two-kingdom views and more of a transformation-alist approach. He certainly articulates several things differently than two-kingdom theologians before him, such as explaining that the antithesis that exists is between worldviews,[37] articulating the commonality between kingdoms in terms of "common grace,"[38] and differentiating between the church as institution (which is limited to specific ecclesiastical matters) and the church as organism (which encompasses all of life for the Chris-tian and extends to any sphere in which he finds himself).[39]

---

34. Jason Lief, "Is Neo-Calvinism Calvinist? A Neo-Calvinist Engagement of Calvin's Two-King-dom Doctrine," *Pro Rege* 27, no. 3 (March 2009): 1–12.
35. Jeremy S. Begbie, "Creation, Christ, and Culture in Dutch Neo-Calvinism," in *Christ in Our Place: The Humanity of God in Christ for the Reconciliation of the World: Essays Presented to Professor James Torrance*, ed. Daniel P. Thimell and Trevor A. Hart (Allison Park, PA: Pickwick, 1989), 126.
36. John Frame, *The Escondido Theology: A Reformed Response to Two Kingdom Theology* (Lakeland, FL: Whitefield Media Productions, 2011), 148n6.
37. Abraham Kuyper, *Lectures on Calvinism* (Grand Rapids: Wm. B. Eerdmans, 1931), 117.
38. Ibid., 168.
39. Abraham Kuyper, "Common Grace," in *Abraham Kuyper: A Centennial Reader*, ed. James D. Bratt (Grand Rapids: Wm. B. Eerdmans, 1998), 194–99.

Where Kuyper especially begins to blur distinctions between the two kingdoms is with his argument that Calvinism is an entire worldview that applies to every aspect of the Christian's life. He resembles the two-kingdom doctrine with his idea of "sphere sovereignty," teaching that each sphere of human activity, including the ecclesiastical and civic, is distinct from every other sphere and exerts no authority over another. But he also argues strongly that Christ exerts lordship over each sphere. Likely his most famous statement articulates his conviction on this point:

> Oh, no single piece of our mental world is to be hermetically sealed off from the rest, and there is not a square inch in the whole domain of our human existence over which Christ, who is Sovereign over *all*, does not cry: "Mine!"[40]

This in itself was no different than Luther and Calvin's beliefs that God instituted and rules the governments of both kingdoms, but where Kuyper begins to be ambiguous is when he discusses how Christians relate in non-ecclesiastical spheres and the relationship between common grace (which accounts for commonality between kingdoms) and special grace (which specifically involves spiritual matters). Kuyper teaches that when a Christian involves himself in civic or cultural matters, he is operating as the organic church in a realm governed by common grace, yet as a Christian who has been influenced by special grace, he can exert that influence of saving grace even upon otherwise common spheres.[41] Carson summarizes Kuyper's point here:

> Because all truth is God's truth, because nothing we legitimately study is unrelated to Christ, Kuyper felt compelled to demonstrate how Christ's sovereignty operates in every sphere. At least during the first half of his career, Kuyper pursued these lines while insisting on the distinctiveness of the church, on the uniqueness of the special grace that Christians alone have received. By setting up a *Christian* university and by establishing a *Christian* trade union and a *Christian* political party, all

---

40. Abraham Kuyper, "Sphere Sovereignty," in *Abraham Kuyper: A Centennial Reader*, 488. Emphasis original.
41. Kuyper, "Common Grace," 194.

the while underlining that Christ is Lord of *all*, he was simultaneously insisting that there is unique insight in the *Christian* revelation and that Christians are mandated to affirm Christ's Lordship in *every* sphere. The result is a vision that emphasizes the uniqueness of the church and of what is now often called special revelation, while equally underscoring the importance of what was later called the cultural mandate.[42]

This allows Kuyper to posit the possibility of a "Christian society," or at least "Christian" aspects of a society.[43] By this he does not mean that every person, or even a majority of persons, in such a society would be a Christian, but rather

> it means that in such a country special grace in the church and among believers exerted so strong a formative influence on common grace that common grace thereby attained its highest development.[44]

VanDrunen sees this way of articulating matters as dangerous since it blurs the dual mediatorship of the Son of God that Calvin formulated. By using "Christian," Kuyper is arguing that the Son is exerting rulership over the civic sphere as "Christ," a title that refers to his redemptive role rather than simply his role as creator. This ambiguity, VanDrunen suggests, leads Kuyper's followers to transition their understanding of the Son's relationship to culture as one of redemption rather than simply creation. Whether Kuyper was a two-kingdom proponent who communicated some of his beliefs ambiguously or an emerging transformationalist, there is no doubt that how he framed the relationship between the church and culture significantly influenced future generations and *did* impact the popularity of the transformationalist approach.

What is particularly interesting in Kuyper's work is that he is the first in the present survey to discuss "culture" *per se*, the idea having only recently reached its present form in the work of Tylor. Prior to Kuyper,

---

42. Carson, *Christ and Culture Revisited*, 214. Emphasis original.
43. Kuyper, "Common Grace," 195.
44. Ibid., 199.

discussions of Christian interaction with unbelievers referred primarily to political, civic, and social issues; Kuyper continues these themes but adds specific reference to culture.

Karl Barth

Ironically, Kuyper's connection between the Son of God as redeemer and culture is seen first not in a follower of Kuyper but in Karl Barth (1886–1968). Barth sharply criticizes the division of Christ's mediatorship into that of creator and redeemer, which he condemns as "the introduction of a foreign god into the sphere of the Church, an attempt to unite Yahweh with Baal, the triune God of Holy Scripture with the concept of being of Aristotelian and Stoic philosophy."[45] Desiring to make everything Christocentric, Barth criticized the two-kingdom model, calling it a system of "double book-keeping,"[46] and argued that everything is under the rule of Christ as redeemer.[47]

Herman Dooyeweerd and North American Neo-Calvinism

The first of Kuyper's direct followers to explicitly transition away from the Reformed doctrine of two kingdoms was Herman Dooyeweerd (1894–1977). Building on Kuyper's ambiguity, and parallel to Barth's own views, Dooyeweerd further develops the idea of worldview as the center of antithesis[48] and roots the Son of God's relationship to cultural matters in redemption rather than in creation.[49] Thus he understands there to be only one kingdom of God in Christ manifested in different spheres. He establishes a new "Christocentric" basis for common grace and develops the Creation-Fall-Redemption paradigm for understanding God and man's work in the world.[50] Involvement in the civic and cultural spheres for Dooyeweerd is redemptive work for the sake of God's kingdom. In fact, he calls for Christians to "strive for the

---

45. Karl Barth, *The Doctrine of God*, ed. G. W. Bromiley and T. F. Torrance, trans. T. H. L Parker et al., vol. 2, Church Dogmatics (Edinburgh: T&T Clark, 1957), 84.
46. Karl Barth, *The Doctrine of Reconciliation*, ed. G. W. Bromiley and T. F. Torrance, trans. G. W. Bromiley, vol. 4, Church Dogmatics [Edinburgh: T&T Clark, 1958], 504.
47. Karl Barth, *The Knowledge of God and the Service of God According to the Teaching of the Reformation*, trans. J. L. M. Haire and Ian Henderson [London: Hodder and Stoughton, 1938], 142–43.
48. Herman Dooyeweerd, *Roots of Western Culture* (Toronto: Wedge, 1979), 5–6, 14–15.
49. Ibid., 137–47.
50. See Dooyeweerd, *Roots of Western Culture*.

consolidation of power in organizations that aim at applying Christian principles to society."[51]

The impact of Dooyeweerd's thoughts cannot be overestimated with relation to the church's responsibility toward culture. Dooyeweerd's heritage is evident especially in North American Neo-Calvinism, largely through the influence of Calvin College in Grand Rapids, Michigan. This begins first with Henry Stob (1908–1996), a student of Dooyeweerd and a professor at Calvin College. Stob agrees with Niehbuhr's categorization of Calvin as a transformationalist and ignores the Christ and Culture in Paradox paradigm altogether.[52] He strongly influenced his students Cornelius Plantinga and Albert Wolters, both who later returned to Calvin College to teach and influenced Craig Bartholomew and Michael Goheen.

---

51. Ibid., 66–67.
52. Henry Stob, *Theological Reflections: Essays on Related Themes* (Grand Rapids: Wm. B. Eerdmans, 1981), 129–30.

chapter 5

HANGING LYRES OR BUILDING

HOUSES: EVALUATION OF

APPROACHES TO CULTURE

Thus says the LORD of hosts, the God of Israel,
to all the exiles whom I have sent into exile from Jerusalem to Babylon:
Build houses and live in them; plant gardens and eat their produce.
Take wives and have sons and daughters;
take wives for your sons, and give your daughters in marriage,
that they may bear sons and daughters;
multiply there, and do not decrease.
Jeremiah 29:4–6

On the one hand, some Hebrews wept and hung up their lyres because they couldn't fathom engaging in cultural activity in a strange land. On the other hand, some Hebrews willingly participated to the degree that they committed idolatry. Surely there is a middle position between these two extremes!

The prophet Jeremiah reveals such a mediating view when he commands God's exiles in Babylon to actively participate in activities such as building houses, planting gardens, enjoying marriage, and bearing children, while avoiding religious syncretism and the idolatry of the foreign nations.

These three responses of Hebrews in captivity provide a helpful illustration of the three primary post-Christendom approaches to culture. This chapter will summarize those approaches and assess their relative strengths and weaknesses.

The Separatist Approach

The Anabaptist approach to culture finds its clearest representation today in the Amish, Mennonites, and Brethren, but other groups manifest the general Christ-against-culture model in various ways as well. Like their forefathers, the Amish and Mennonites concern themselves not with national or cultural identity with others around them but rather "on honoring their parents for their faithfulness in recovering and preserving the faith of the Anabaptist forebears."[1] James Juhnke summarizes the typical Anabaptist position, specifically related to political involvement, as expressed in modern day Mennonites:

> The traditional Anabaptist-Mennonite position, shaped by the persistent theological distinction between church and state and by a history of governmental persecution, is one of noninvolvement in political affairs.[2]

The Mennonites, however, began a slight compromise in areas of voting and office-holding in the early 1800s,[3] while the Amish have maintained a more thorough separatist approach.

There has also been a rise in recent years of a group identified as Neo-Anabaptists, who continue to perpetuate the separatist two-kingdom approach of their namesake. Authors in this group include Harold Bender (*The Anabaptist Vision*), John Howard Yoder (*Authentic Transformation: A New Vision of Christ and Culture*), Stanley Hauerwas (*The Myth of a Christian Nation: How the Quest for Political Power Is Destroying the Church*), Shane Claiborne (*Jesus for President: Politics for Ordinary Radicals*), and

---

1. Juhnke, *A People of Two Kingdoms*, 1.
2. Ibid., 4.
3. Ibid., 11.

many of the emergent church authors. These Neo-Anabaptists specifically denounce American Christianity for what they claim is its capitulation to the American political system, argue that the church is a community rather than an institution, and advocate social reform.

The greatest strength of the separatist position is its recognition of inherent corruption in the world's system and its insistence upon complete separation from that world. However, some of its descendants have extended these principles to include all parts of human culture, leading groups like the Amish toward an extreme isolationism and some Neo-Anabaptists toward a sort of liberal socialism. Nevertheless, the Anabaptist position could legitimately be considered a slight modification of the two-kingdom approach.

The Two-Kingdom Approach

The two-kingdom approach is essentially built upon two ideas: natural law, and a clear distinction between redemptive and non-redemptive social spheres. The first idea is built on passages like Romans 2:14–15 and the assumption that moral norms are inscribed on the hearts of all men. These norms are the basis for common society of which both believers and unbelievers are members. They are not salvific in any way but rather provide for human peace even among the unregenerate. This general civic realm is not all that exists, however, since there also exists salvific revelation beyond this common natural law; two-kingdom advocates sharply distinguish between believers and unbelievers and also between the ecclesiastical government and the civic government. Believers are governed not only by natural law but also by a saving knowledge of Jesus Christ, his person, and his works. But while a person can be a member of only one city (to use Augustine's term), a believer has dual membership in both kingdoms and thus submits himself to both governments, each of which has been created by God to order the world. Whether or not Calvin advocated a two-kingdom or transformationalist approach, he summarizes this perspective particularly well:

> This, then, is the distinction: that there is one kind of understanding of earthly things; another of heavenly. I call "earthly things" those which do not pertain to God or his Kingdom, to true justice, or to the blessedness of the future life; but which

have their significance and relationship with regard to the present life and are, in a sense, confined within its bounds. I call
"heavenly things" the pure knowledge of God, the nature of
true righteousness, and the mysteries of the Heavenly Kingdom. The first class includes government, household manage-
ment, all mechanical skills, and the liberal arts. In the second
are the knowledge of God and of his will, and the rule by which
we conform our lives to it.[4]

These two kingdoms rule their respective spheres separately and do not
overlap. Christians, as members of both kingdoms, operate fully under
the laws of each. As a member of the heavenly kingdom, a Christian
submits to the Word of God; as a member of the earthly kingdom, he
submits to human laws.

The two-kingdom theology is expressed most popularly today by
Michael Horton (*Where in the World Is the Church? A Christian View of
Culture and Your Role in It*), D. G. Hart (*Secular Faith: Why Christianity
Favors the Separation of Church and State*), Jason Stellman (*Dual Citizens:
Worship and Life between the Already and the Not Yet*), and David Van-
Drunen (*Natural Law and the Two Kingdoms: A Study in the Development
of Reformed Social Thought; Living in God's Two Kingdoms: A Biblical Vi-
sion for Christianity and Culture*).

Perhaps the most recent popular articulation of two-kingdom thought
is David VanDrunen's *Living in God's Two Kingdoms*. He disagrees with
the typical transformationalist motifs of "creation regained" and the "cultural mandate" by insisting that these have been accomplished in Christ
as the second Adam and are therefore not the responsibility of the church.
Instead of focusing on "creation regained," VanDrunen suggests that
Christians can celebrate "re-creation gained" as a work accomplished in
Jesus Christ.[5] This does not mean that Christians will not be active in
culture, it simply removes the eschatological or "creation mandate" mo-
tivations. He argues that Christians are to live as sojourners in this life as
part of two distinct kingdoms and explores practical ways this thinking
will affect church ministry and Christian living.

---

4. Calvin, *Institutes*, 1.2.2.13.
5. David VanDrunen, *Living in God's Two Kingdoms: A Biblical Vision for Christianity and Culture* (Wheaton: Crossway, 2010), 26.

The two-kingdom approach thus avoids the triumphalism that can sometimes characterize the transformationalists. It has no aspirations to transform society but rather claims to have a more realistic understanding of the fallenness of the world. It also protects the regular, God-ordained operations of the church governed by explicit biblical commands. So while Christians can and should be actively involved in the civic realm, the church itself is limited only to those matters expressly prescribed in Scripture.

The two-kingdom approach has come under criticism from a number of sources, however. First, this view can give the impression that God has no place in the public sphere. Despite Luther's insistence that God ordained and rules through both kingdoms, a sharp distinction between them may lead Christians to fail to recognize the necessity to do all to God's glory, even outside the gatherings of the church. Separation of church and state may very easily become separation of Christianity from life. As Carson points out, "What this vision rightly captures is the tension . . . but it is easy so to polarize the two kingdoms that we forget that one God stands over all."[6] Second, the idea of natural law sometimes gives the impression of a neutral middle ground between believers and unbelievers. Thus while the two-kingdom approach preserves a distinction between kingdoms, the antithesis may be blurred with the idea of natural law.

The Transformationalist Approach

The third post-Christendom approach to culture is the one kingdom, or transformationalist, posture. This position appeals to the redemption motif in Scripture, namely that God desires to redeem all of his creation and that the church is already involved in that process through cultural redemption. This, transformationalists argue, is a continuation of the creation mandate (Gen. 1:28) that was interrupted by the Fall, and thus the Great Commission is essentially a continuation of that original mandate this side of the cross. Thus they deny any real sacred/secular distinction; for the transformationalist, all of life is worship. Although they recognize antithesis between the values of Christianity and the values of the world's system, they nevertheless tend to emphasize common grace, which gives all of culture a neutral, or even positive, framework for engagement. They

---

6. Carson, *Christ and Culture Revisited*, 211.

accomplish this through a distinction between worldview and culture. The worldviews of believers and unbelievers are at complete odds with one another, but the cultural material they use to express their worldviews is neutral in itself. Cornelius Plantinga summarizes this perspective well: "All has been created good, including the full range of human cultures that emerge when humans act according to God's design."[7]

Those defending this position typically classify themselves as Reformed followers of John Calvin through the thinking of Abraham Kuyper. Of course, as the historical survey above illustrates, there are those in the Reformed camps who insist that the transformationalists have departed from the teachings of both Calvin and Kuyper, which is why the monikers "Neo-Calvinist" or "Neo-Kuyperian" are used to describe them. Popular defenders of variations of the transformationalist position include Cornelius Plantinga (*Engaging God's World: A Christian Vision of Faith, Learning, and Living*), Albert Wolters (*Creation Regained: Biblical Basics for a Reformational Worldview*), and Michael Goheen (*Living at the Crossroads: An Introduction to Christian Worldview*).

Perhaps one of the most popular and influential proponents of the transformationalist approach is Albert Wolters, who seeks to articulate a "reformational worldview" in *Creation Regained: Biblical Basics for a Reformational Worldview*. Wolters very much reflects Kuyper in the aim of his book, which he states "is an attempt to spell out the content of a biblical worldview and its significance for our lives as we seek to be obedient to the Scripture."[8] This is not just any "biblical worldview," however; Wolters specifically calls it "reformational" and in particular ties his understanding to the Dutch reformed movement. Essential to his "reformational worldview" is the idea that all the scriptural concepts of salvation apply not just to individuals but to the entire creation:

> The reformational worldview takes all the key terms in this ecumenical Trinitarian confession in a universal, all-encompassing sense. The terms "reconciled," "created," "fallen," "world," "renews," and "Kingdom of God" are held to be cosmic in scope.

---

7. Cornelius J. Plantinga, *Engaging God's World: A Christian Vision of Faith, Learning, and Living* (Grand Rapids: Wm. B. Eerdmans, 2002), 10–11.

8. Albert M. Wolters, *Creation Regained: Biblical Basics for a Reformational Worldview*, 2nd ed. (Grand Rapids: Wm. B. Eerdmans, 2005), 1.

> In principle, nothing apart from God himself falls outside the range of these foundational realities of biblical religion.[9]

He repudiates what he calls the "dualistic worldview," which distinguishes between "sacred" and "secular." Instead, Wolters's primary thesis is that "the redemption in Jesus Christ means the *restoration* of an original good creation" in its entirety.[10]

Wolters explores the transformationalist motif of creation, fall, and redemption, developed first by Herman Dooyeweerd. Creation, Wolters argues, is "the correlation of the sovereign activity of the Creator and the created order," and thus it is intrinsically good.[11] This truism extends beyond simply what God has directly created to "the structures of society, to the world of art, to business and commerce. Human civilization is *normed* throughout. ... There is nothing in human life that does not belong to the created order."[12] In fact, the original creation was essentially empty, and

> people must now carry on the work of development: by being fruitful they must fill it even more; by subduing it they must form it even more. Mankind, as God's representatives on earth, carry on where God left off.[13]

This objective is known as the "creation mandate." Wolters claims that the history of mankind has been a progressive "unfolding" of God's desire for the universe. He argues that despite sin, man's cultural production will climax one day in "a new heaven and a new earth" that will maintain an "essential continuity with our experience now."[14] Thus Wolters argues for an essential goodness of creation, including later human cultural developments.

Although creation itself—and by extension culture—is inherently good, mankind's fall into sin did have consequences, what Wolters describes as "catastrophic significance for creation as a whole."[15] Sin created the possibility of perversion of God's creation. However, he is quick to insist that "sin

---

9. Ibid., 11.
10. Ibid., 12. Emphasis original.
11. Ibid., 14.
12. Ibid., 25. Emphasis original.
13. Ibid., 41.
14. Ibid., 48.
15. Ibid., 53.

neither abolishes nor becomes identified with creation." Rather, it "introduces an entirely new dimension to the created order."[16] In order to explain
the relationship between the intrinsically good creation and the effects of
sin, Wolters introduces the ideas of "structure" and "direction." Structure
"refers to the order of creation," the basic "nature" created by God and is
thus inherently good.[17] Direction is a relationship toward or away from God.
"Anything in creation," according to Wolters, "can be directed either toward
or away from God—that is, directed either in obedience or disobedience to
his law."[18] The structure of creation itself presents limits as to how warped it
can be turned, which is what Wolters describes as "common grace."

This framework allows him to discuss elements in culture that in
themselves are rooted in the created order (structure) but nevertheless
have been used in ways contrary to God's will (direction). Creation, Wolters argues, was made good, but since the fall mankind has directed various elements of creation away from God, God's desire is to redeem these
elements and redirect them. He argues that "dualists" often reject the
structure instead of simply dealing with its direction.

The "reformational worldview," according to Wolters, seeks to redeem
elements whose structures are rooted in the created order and thus good
but whose direction has been warped by fallen mankind. "The original
good creation is to be restored."[19] This, according to Wolters, extends to
all realms of human development including marriage, emotions, sexual-
ity, politics, art, and business. This is God's plan, insists Wolters, and
it is also the mission of all Christians: "The obvious implication is that
the new humanity (God's people) is called to promote renewal in every
department of creation."[20] Thus for the transformationalist, all cultural
activity is kingdom work.[21]

Wolters's perspective well summarizes the transformationalist view.
The strength of this model is that it recognizes the inherent goodness of
God's original creation as well as the mandate for God's people to be ac-
tive in his world, cultivating what he has given them and actively living

---

16. Ibid., 57.
17. Ibid., 59.
18. Ibid.
19. Ibid., 71.
20. Ibid., 73.
21. See Plantinga, *Engaging God's World*, 109–13.

out their faith in every sphere of life. But Wolters's book also demonstrates most transformationalists' failure to recognize several key distinctions in their argumentation. First, Wolters fails to distinguish between God's creation and man's creation. He often conflates the two categories, equating the intrinsic goodness of God's handiwork with what mankind produces. He is correct that everything God creates is intrinsically good and that even the act of human creation is a good thing. However, to insist that every product of man's hand is therefore also intrinsically good is to slide dangerously close to Pelagianism.

Second, Wolters fails to distinguish between what might be called elements and their forms. He may be correct in that the basic elements of human civilization are good, but the forms they take may be intrinsically evil. His structure/direction categories have the potential of helping to distinguish between elements (structure) and forms (direction), but he often fails to do so by miscategorizing forms as elements. He lists several different "structures" that Christians may face, but some of what he lists is really the form (the direction) of a more basic element (structure). For example, he lists technology as a structure, but technology is already a direction itself; it is a form of the more basic element of communication. The same is true for dance and music. In short, Wolters's structure/direction categories are a good starting point, but the situation is often more complex.

The problem with a failure to recognize such distinctions is that the transformationalist position eventually understands culture in general to be neutral. Any "sinful direction" it recognizes is typically limited to the content of a given cultural form but not the form itself. Rather, since forms are characterized as elements (or directions as structures), very few if any cultural forms are judged to be against God's law. The danger of this view is that anything in culture is fair game for the Christian, and "cultural redemption" means little more than adoption and reorientation of cultural forms that are themselves sinful. Andy Crouch astutely observes where the transformationalist approach has often led: "The rise of interest in cultural transformation has been accompanied by a rise in cultural transformation of a different sort—the transformation of the church into the culture's image."[22]

---

22. Andy Crouch, *Culture Making: Recovering Our Creative Calling* (Downers Grove, IL: InterVarsity Press, 2008), 189.

The Missional Approach

The missional church movement is certainly not a monolithic group, yet characteristics of this movement are strikingly similar to distinctives of the transformationalist approach to culture. Several authors have suggested that the missional church movement is essentially transformationalist, including Michael Goheen[23] and Mark Snoeberger.[24] Like transformationalists, missionalists see no sacred/secular distinction and argue that all of life is worship. Like transformationalists, missional authors recognize antithesis between the church and its surrounding culture, but also like transformationalists, their initial posture is one of acceptance, and even when certain aspects of culture are contrary to Scripture, their method is to adopt the form and renegotiate its meaning. Goheen argues that this was essentially Lesslie Newbigin's objective.[25] They see cultural forms in and of themselves as neutral—even good; it is only particular uses of those forms that distort them: "The gospel speaks a Yes and a No to each cultural form—yes to the creational structure and no to the idolatrous distortion."[26] Goheen suggests that Newbigin "sought to forge a theory of contextualization in the way of creation, sin, and redemption."[27]

This theme of cultural redemption is seen in other missional advocates after Newbigin. For example, Alan Hirsch expresses the importance of incarnational ministry in the objective of cultural redemption:

> By acting incarnationally, missionaries ensure that the people of any given tribe embrace the gospel and live it out in ways that are *meaningful* to their tribe. The culture as a whole thus finds its completion and redemption in Jesus. The gospel thus transforms the tribe *from the inside*, so to speak. We are reminded in Revelation 21–22 that in the great redemption there will be

---

23. Michael Goheen, "Is Lesslie Newbigin's Model of Contextualization Anticultural?," *Mission Studies* 19, no. 1/2 (January 1, 2002): 136–56.
24. Mark A. Snoeberger, "History, Ecclesiology, and Mission, Or, Are We Missing Some Options Here?" (Unpublished, Detroit Baptist Theological Seminary, n.d.), http://www.dbts.edu/pdf/macp/2010/Snoeberger,%20History%20Ecclesiology%20and%20Mission.pdf; accessed November 30, 2012.
25. Goheen, "Is Lesslie Newbigin's Model of Contextualization Anticultural?".
26. Michael Goheen and Albert M. Wolters, "Worldview between Story and Mission," in Wolters, *Creation Regained*, 140.
27. Goheen, "Is Lesslie Newbigin's Model of Contextualization Anticultural?".

> a genuine expression of redeemed culture as people from every
> tribe and language group and nation will give praise to God for
> what he has done for them. It is from within their own cultural
> expressions that the nations will worship.[28]

What is clear from this missional statement of cultural redemption is
that Hirsch does not see "redemption" here as "transformation" in any
real sense. Since, according to Hirsch, the nations will worship "from
within their own cultural expressions," the nations do not need to—even
must not—change their cultural forms when they come to Christ. Rather,
"cultural redemption" merely means that redeemed people continue to
participate in the same cultural forms they did before their redemption,
only this time adapted for Christian use.

Craig Van Gelder also uses "redemption" language—specifically the
Neo-Kuyperian "creation-fall-redemption" theme—to describe the missional approach to culture:

> The Old Testament story is about creation, fall, redemption,
> and the expectation of the day of the Lord. God's passion for
> the world is made clear throughout this story. The whole world
> was created to be in relationship with God, but the fall dev-
> astated the design. After humanity's fall into sin, the story of
> redemption unfolds around God's continuing concern for the
> entire world. This is made clear through the various covenants
> that God initiated with the human community.[29]

Van Gelder's statement reveals the deep connection between missional
thinking and the transformationalist approach to culture, namely, that
the missional principle of *missio Dei* is itself intrinsically transformationalist. Snoeberger makes this point, identifying Barth as an important influence in this regard:

> Nowhere is this idea more evident than in his concept of the
> *missio Dei*. Our Trinitarian God, for Barth, was by nature a

---

28. Hirsch, *The Forgotten Ways*, 138. Emphasis original.
29. Craig Van Gelder, *The Ministry of the Missional Church: A Community Led by the Spirit* (Grand Rapids: Baker Books, 2007), 89.

sending God with a singular mission which the church shares. This mission is embodied in Christ and participated in by the similarly sent-out church. God is not merely redeeming his elect, but is also redeeming all creation—these two "missions" cannot, in fact, properly be distinguished. It is impossible to overstate the influence of this model on modern missiology.[30]

Missional advocates teach that God has a mission to redeem all of creation. The Missional Manifesto articulates this: "By nature, God is the 'sending one' who initiates the redemption of his whole creation."[31] This alone is not necessarily evidence of transformationalism, but missional teaching takes an additional step by arguing that God's mission and the church's mission are one and the same; thus embedded in *missio Dei* is the belief that the church's mission is the redemption of creation, essentially a transformationalist view. It is therefore not surprising that advocates of the transformationalist approach, such as Nicholas Wolterstorff, also use *missio Dei* language: "We are not to stand around, hands folded, waiting for shalom to arrive. We are workers in God's cause, his peace-workers. The *missio Dei* is our mission."[32]

These similarities may be coincidental, but certainly intersections between the proponents of both the missional and transformationalist perspectives imply otherwise. Of particular interest is the relationship between Karl Barth and Lesslie Newbigin. Hunsberger notes that "the large familiarity with Barth's work which Newbigin shows in his writings indicates a marked appreciation for Barth's contribution."[33] Both served together on committees of the World Council of Churches from 1949 onward. Both also root their ecclesiology in the *missio Dei*. While Newbigin certainly differs from Barth on a number of theological issues, he essentially agreed with him in matters related to the kingdom, culture, mission, and ecclesiology in general. In fact, Michael Goheen, an advocate of both the missional church movement and transformationalism,

30. Snoeberger, "History, Ecclesiology, and Mission," 9.
31. http://www.missionalmanifesto.com; accessed October 4, 2014.
32. Nicholas Wolterstorff, *Until Justice and Peace Embrace: The Kuyper Lectures for 1981 Delivered at the Free University of Amsterdam* (Grand Rapids: Wm. B. Eerdmans, 1983), 68.
33. George Hunsberger, *Bearing the Witness of the Spirit: Lesslie Newbigin's Theology of Cultural Plurality* (Grand Rapids: Wm. B. Eerdmans, 1998), 209.

argues that Newbigin was a transformationalist himself: "In his treatment of the various public domains of western culture (politics, science) Newbigin gives consideration to faith as an agent of cultural reformation."[34] He insists that although cultural forms are corrupted by sin, their essence remains good because of God's intent to redeem creation:

> Every custom, institution, and practice of culture is corrupted by sin; yet the goodness of the creational structure remains because of God's faithfulness to creation. This means that culture is redeemable; it also provides a strategy for cultural involvement.[35]

One cannot help but notice Wolters's language of "creational structure" in Goheen's description of Newbigin's views. Notably, Goheen wrote a postscript for the second edition of *Creation Regained*, and Wolters expresses his own indebtedness to Newbigin.[36]

From these similarities and intersections, it appears that the missional approach to culture is a combination of Barthian and Neo-Calvinist ecclesiology. In other words, the missional church movement is essentially transformationalist.

There are at least two problems with the approach to culture advocated by practical missional authors. First, because their understanding of culture comes essentially from the prevailing anthropological model, their underlying assumption of cultural neutrality all but obliterates any notion of cultural antithesis. Without the antithesis, there is nothing to transform; thus missional practitioners do not really transform culture, they adopt it—they do not redeem culture, they reorient it.

This quasi-transformationalist perspective has therefore shifted the missional approach from the early articulations to how it is actually practiced today. The earliest missional advocates sought to distinguish between the gospel and western culture, which they believed had merged with Christendom. But the transformational impulse imbedded in the concept of *missio Dei* itself is rooted in Christendom ideas. Van Gelder admits as much:

---

34. Goheen, "Is Lesslie Newbigin's Model of Contextualization Anticultural?," 138.
35. Ibid., 150.
36. Wolters, *Creation Regained*, ix.

The understanding of what we refer to today as "God's mission" was developed in these confessional documents within a world-view of Christendom in which the church was established by the state. It was thus assumed that the church was responsible for the world, with the church's direct involvement defined primarily in terms of the magistrate's obligation to carry out Christian duties on behalf of the church in the world. Within a Christendom worldview, the church and the world occupied the same location: the social reality of the church represented the same social reality of the world within that particular context.[37]

Thus, more recent missional authors are falling back into the error they supposedly repudiate. Instead of advocating Christ as the transformer of culture, they are viewing Christ above culture once again. They are accommodating culture and seeking to merge Christ and culture rather than seeking real transformation. Their understanding of *missio Dei*, culture, and incarnation are actually expressions of the Enlightenment and Christendom ideas they claim to reject.

---

37. Craig Van Gelder and Dwight J. Zscheile, *The Missional Church in Perspective: Mapping Trends and Shaping the Conversation* (Grand Rapids: Baker Academic, 2011), 19.

chapter 6

SONGS, HOUSES, AND GARDENS:

WHAT IS CULTURE, ANYWAY?

Keep your conduct among the Gentiles honorable,
so that when they speak against you as evildoers,
they may see your good deeds
and glorify God on the day of visitation.
1 Peter 2:12

I have argued that the worship philosophy of the missional church movement is rooted in a particular errant understanding of culture and contextualization. These ideas of culture and contextualization were shaped
primarily by secular anthropology, causing the missional movement to lack
a robust biblical framework for their application of the ideas to worship
philosophy and practice. This chapter will construct such a biblical framework of culture and contextualization by exploring how the New Testament
treats subjects nearly equivalent to the contemporary definitions of culture
and contextualization as expressed by secular anthropology.

Since cultural anthropology formulated the common understanding of
culture, and since the term "culture" is not a biblical one, there is little reason to debate the definition itself. Rather, what is important for Christians
concerned with culture is to determine, taking for granted the anthropological definition of culture, what ideas in Scripture may inform their un-

derstanding of culture. At least three separate categories of New Testament Greek terms possibly parallel the more contemporary idea of culture.

Terms Associated with Ethnic Identity

The first grouping includes terms translated with the English words "race," "tribe," "nation," "people" or "languages." These ideas are probably the most commonly cited by missional authors who are seeking to justify cultural neutrality. For example, Driscoll equates "race," "nation," and "culture," alluding to Revelation 7:9 when he insists that "God promised that people from every race, culture, language, and nation will be present to worship him as their culture follows them into heaven."[1]

The term representative of this group that Christian anthropologists mostly cite is *ethnos*. For example, in commenting on Matthew 28:16–20, Christian cultural anthropologists Paris and Howell explain that "the word translated 'nations' here (*ethnos*) refers to the culture of a people, an ethnic group."[2] They directly equate *ethnos* with culture and insist that "cultural anthropology helps us fulfill the Great Commission by preparing Christians to go to all *ethnē* and speak and live effectively."[3] Stetzer likewise defines *ethnos* in terms of "people groups, population segments, and cultural environments."[4] Additionally, the popularity of terms such as "ethnodoxology" among missional worship advocates reveals the assumption that this New Testament term proves the necessity of a multicultural approach to worship.

Of the 164 times it appears in the New Testament, *ethnos* is translated in the ESV as "Gentile" ninety-six times, "nation" sixty-eight times, "pagans" three times, and "people" two times. Lexicons define the term as "a multitude (whether of men or of beasts) associated or living together, ... a multitude of individuals of the same nature or genus, ... a race, nation, people group,"[5] or even specifically link it to the idea of culture: "a peo-

---

1. Driscoll, *Radical Reformission*, 100.
2. Paris and Howell, *Introducing Cultural Anthropology*, 23.
3. Ibid.
4. Stetzer and Putman, *Breaking the Missional Code*, 37–38.
5. James Strong, *The Exhaustive Concordance of the Bible: Showing Every Word of the Text of the Common English Version of the Canonical Books, and Every Occurrence of Each Word in Regular Order, Together with Dictionaries of the Hebrew and Greek Words of the Original, with References to the English Words* (Peabody, MA: Hendrickson, 2004).

ple, a large group based on various cultural, physical or geographic ties."[6] Lexicons do not define *ethnos* as culture itself, however, but rather identify culture as one element that unites an *ethnos*, as in Bullinger, who defines the term as "a number of people living together bound together by like habits and customs; then generally people, tribe, nation, with reference to the connection with each other rather than the separation from others by descent, language or constitution."[7]

Indeed, the term is used to designate groups of people who identify with common values. Missional authors assume that New Testament authors use *ethnos* as a parallel to "culture," yet this correspondence falls outside the common usage of the term. An *ethnos* may be united by shared culture, but it is not the same as culture. Hiebert agrees: "*Nation (ethnos)* means a community of people held together by the same laws, customs, and mutual interests."[8] The term refers to the group of people, not to the culture around which the group unites.

Furthermore, use of the term in the New Testament is normally intended to *blur cultural differences* rather than to highlight them. For example, the two passages cited above by missional writers use *ethnos* most clearly to signify something broader than the contemporary notion of culture. In Matthew 28:19, Jesus commands his followers to "teach all nations [*ethnos*]." Carson suggests that Matthew "uses *ethnē* in its basic sense of 'tribes,' 'nations,' or 'peoples' and means 'all peoples [without distinction]' or 'all nations [without distinction].'"[9] The point of the command is not, necessarily, to emphasize the cross-cultural reality of evangelizing each distinct cultural group; rather "the aim of Jesus' disciples … is to make disciples of all men everywhere, without distinction."[10]

The other passage often cited by missional authors to prove that every culture is legitimate since people from every nation will be admitted into heaven is Revelation 5:9: "And they sang a new song, saying, 'Worthy are

---

6. James Swanson, *Dictionary of Biblical Languages with Semantic Domains: Greek (New Testament)*, electronic ed. (Oak Harbor, WA: Logos Research Systems, Inc., 1997).

7. Ethelbert William Bullinger, *A Critical Lexicon and Concordance to the English and Greek New Testament: Together with an Index of Greek Words, and Several Appendices* (London: Longmans Green, 1908), 316.

8. D. Edmond Hiebert, *First Peter* (Chicago: Moody Press, 1984), 134.

9. Frank E. Gaebelein, ed., *The Expositor's Bible Commentary, Volume 8: Matthew, Mark, Luke* (Grand Rapids: Zondervan Publishing House, 1984), 596.

10. Ibid.

you to take the scroll and to open its seals, for you were slain, and by your blood you ransomed people for God from every tribe [*phylēs*] and language [*glōssēs*] and people [*laou*] and nation [*ethnous*].'"[11] Here John uses four terms related to ethnic identity, but once again, John uses the terms not to emphasize cultural distinctions between various people groups but rather to signify all peoples without national or cultural distinctions. For example, Mounce states of the terms in this verse, "It is fruitless to attempt a distinction between these terms as ethnic, linguistic, political, etc. The Seer is stressing the universal nature of the church and for this purpose piles up phrases for their rhetorical value."[12] Likewise, Thomas argues, "The enumeration includes representatives of every nationality, without distinction of race, geographical location, or political persuasion."[13] These conclusions regarding the use of *ethnos* apply equally to nearly synonymous terms in Revelation 5:9 such as *phylē* ("tribe"), *glōssa* ("language"), and *laos* ("people"). Indeed, the New Testament perspective on race seems to be that of eliminating racial distinctions rather than highlighting them. The use of another term related to race, *Hellēn* ("Greek"), illustrates this point. According to Paul, in Christ there is no distinction between Jew and Greek (Gal 3:28). Rather, all are united into one newly distinct body.

These examples of the use of terms related to ethnic identity by New Testament authors indicate that the terms signify distinct groups of people that unify around common heritage, geographical location, language, and/or custom. "Culture" as defined by contemporary anthropologists may be one of the elements around which an *ethnos* unifies, but an *ethnos* is not "culture" itself. Similarly, *phylē* is not a lineage, it is a people united by lineage; likewise, although *glōssa* is often used to specifically designate languages, in these cases it is used metaphorically to signify people united by a common language; in the same way *laos* and *ethnos* identify groups united by politics or culture, but they do not equal culture itself.

The implication here is twofold. First, the "culture" of a people is not arbitrary; groups unite around shared beliefs, values, and lineage, which in turn produce a culture that is characteristic of the group. Second, contrary to some missional authors, the New Testament does not indicate that all *cultures* will be present in the eschaton but rather that all *kinds of people*

11. These same four terms appear also in 7:9, 11:9, 13:7, and 14:6.
12. Robert H. Mounce, *The Book of Revelation* (Grand Rapids: Wm. B. Eerdmans, 1998), 136.
13. Robert Thomas, *Revelation 1–7 Commentary* (Chicago: Moody Publishers, 1992), 401.

regardless of distinctions will be present. This alone does not discredit the position of cultural neutrality, but appealing to terms of ethnicity and their relationship to salvation and the life to come cannot prove the position.

Terms Related to "the World"

The second category of New Testament terms that may indicate a parallel with the contemporary idea of "culture" includes words related to the "world order." These terms include *aiōn* ("age," "world") and *kosmos* ("world"). They can refer to the physical earth, people in general, or a period of time. However, at least three passages in particular use these terms in ways that might be construed as parallel to the anthropological idea of culture, especially by those who consider culture to be an inherently evil influence.

The first is John 17:14–16:

> I have given them your word, and the world [*kosmos*] has hated them because they are not of the world [*kosmou*], just as I am not of the world [*kosmou*]. I do not ask that you take them out of the world [*kosmou*], but that you keep them from the evil one. They are not of the world [*kosmou*], just as I am not of the world [*kosmou*].

Here *kosmos* is being used to identify an identifiable world-system. In this context John asserts several conclusions about the "world": (1) Christ is not "of" it, (2) believers are not "of" it, but they are "in" it, and (3) the "evil one" is in some way related to it. While this seems to have a connection with the contemporary idea of culture, this system includes the values and orientation that create culture but does not appear to identify culture itself as defined by anthropologists.

A related passage is 1 John 2:15–17. Here *kosmos* is treated decidedly negatively:

> Do not love the world [*kosmon*] or the things in the world [*kosmō*]. If anyone loves the world [*kosmon*], the love of the Father is not in him. For all that is in the world [*kosmō*]—the desires of the flesh and the desires of the eyes and pride of life—is not from the Father but is from the world [*kosmou*].

And the world [*kosmos*] is passing away along with its desires,
but whoever does the will of God abides forever.

Barket notes that John uses *kosmos* here far differently than he did in John
3:16: "Here, however, the world is presented as the evil system totally under
the grip of the devil (cf. 1 John 5:19; John 12:31; 14:30). It is the 'godless world' (NEB), the world of 'emptiness and evil,' the world of enmity
against God (James 4:4)."[14] Once again, however, this world-system does
not appear to be the same thing as what anthropologists call culture. Not all
of what mankind produces is godless, empty, or at enmity with God.

The final passage is Romans 12:2. This time the term in question is
aiōn, and once again this term is treated negatively:

Do not be conformed to this world [*aiōni*], but be transformed
by the renewal of your mind, that by testing you may discern
what is the will of God, what is good and acceptable and perfect.

The term appears to be used nearly synonymously here with how John
used *kosmos* in John 14 and 1 John 2: it describes a world-system to which
believers are not to be conformed. But once again, the term appears to
signify an ordered system of values alienated from God rather than signifying culture itself. David Wells defines at least one use of the term
kosmos as "the ways in which fallen aspirations are given public expression
in any given culture."[15] He argues that when used in this sense, the New
Testament "is speaking of that system of values which takes root in any
given culture, the system of values that arises from fallen human nature,
and which for that reason marginalizes (pushes to the periphery) God, his
truth, and his Christ."[16] He continues:

Worldliness is all in a society that validates the fallenness within us. Worldliness is everything in our culture that makes sin
look normal and which makes righteousness look strange and

14. Frank E. Gaebelein, ed., *The Expositor's Bible Commentary, Volume 12: Hebrews through Rev-
    elation* (Grand Rapids: Zondervan Publishing House, 1981), 321.
15. David F. Wells, "Marketing the Church: Analysis and Assessment," *Faith and Mission* 12, no.
    2 (Spring 1995): 15.
16. Ibid.

bizarre. Worldliness is that which says it's okay to be self-righteous, self-centered, self-satisfied, self-aggrandizing, and self-promoting. Those things are all okay, our culture says. Then it says that those who pursue self-denial or self-effacement for Christ's sake are stupid. That is worldliness—how life appears from this fallen center within myself, this center which has taken the place of God and of his truth. That, I take it, is what the New Testament has in view when it speaks about worldliness. It is talking about a cultural phenomenon, about the public environment by which we are surrounded, that which validates all that is fallen within us. It is what we encounter in movies, in television, in the workplace, in the people with whom we rub shoulders. We hear it in conversations; we see it in advertisements; it is in the air all the time.[17]

Therefore, assuming the anthropological definition of culture as the entire way of life of a people, the idea of "world" does not directly apply in these cases since "world" is something entirely hostile to God in every case, while certainly not everything a people does is evil.

Terms Related to Behavior

A third category of New Testament terms that could parallel the contemporary concept of culture relate to behavior, including words most often translated as "behavior," "conduct," or "way of life."

Among these, New Testament authors most often use *anastrophē* in this manner. Bullinger defines the word as "life, as made up of actions; mode of life, conduct, deportment."[18] The Apostle Paul uses it to describe his behavior in his previous existence: "For you have heard of my former life [*anastrophēn*] in Judaism, how I persecuted the church of God violently and tried to destroy it" (Gal. 1:13). Boice notes of Paul's use of the term here:

The word Paul used for his former "way of life" (*anastrophē*) is singularly appropriate to the Jewish faith. Judaism was not

17. Ibid.
18. Bullinger, *A Critical Lexicon and Concordance to the English and Greek New Testament*, 186.

a mask to be donned or doffed at will, as was the case with so many of the pagan religions. Judaism was a way of life, involving all of life, and Paul is correct in describing it as his exclusive sphere of existence before his conversion.[19]

Paul understood his way of life as flowing directly and necessarily from his religious convictions and values. Because of this perspective, Paul insisted that one's conduct must change with conversion:

> Now this I say and testify in the Lord, that you must no longer walk as the Gentiles [*ethnē*] do, in the futility of their minds. They are darkened in their understanding, alienated from the life of God because of the ignorance that is in them, due to their hardness of heart. They have become callous and have given themselves up to sensuality, greedy to practice every kind of impurity. But that is not the way you learned Christ!—assuming that you have heard about him and were taught in him, as the truth is in Jesus, to put off your old self, which belongs to your former manner of life [*anastrophēn*] and is corrupt through deceitful desires, and to be renewed in the spirit of your minds, and to put on the new self, created after the likeness of God in true righteousness and holiness. (Eph. 4:17–24)

Here Paul distinguishes between behavior of the *ethnē* and the behavior of Christ-followers. He notes that the values of the former ("futility of their minds," "darkened understanding," "alienation from the life of God," "ignorance," and "hardness of heart") lead to sinful behavior ("sensuality," "greed," and "impurity"). He describes this once again as their "former manner of life," using the term *anastrophē*. In contrast, the new values of Christians ("renewed in the spirit of your minds") produce a new way of life ("put on the new self, created after the likeness of God in true righteousness and holiness"). Paul communicates a similar sentiment to Timothy when he admonishes, "Set the believers an example in speech, in conduct [*anastrophē*], in love, in faith, in purity" (1 Tim. 4:12). Paul

---

19. Frank E. Gaebelein, gen. ed., *The Expositor's Bible Commentary, Volume 10: Romans through Galatians* (Grand Rapids: Zondervan Publishing House, 1976), 433.

clearly uses *anastrophēn*, therefore, to describe a particular way of life, whether good or evil, that flows from religious beliefs and values. Boice summarizes:

> Paul now gives the content of the teaching his readers received, though the verb is not actually repeated. Their previous life style was to be discarded completely. They must forsake their old behavioral haunts (*anastrophē;* NIV, "your former way of life") and indeed lay aside the costume of their unregenerate selves.[20]

The most prolific use of *anastrophē* occurs in Peter's writings. Forms of the term appear three times in 1 Peter 1:13–19:

> Therefore, preparing your minds for action, and being sober-minded, set your hope fully on the grace that will be brought to you at the revelation of Jesus Christ. As obedient children, do not be conformed to the passions of your former ignorance, but as he who called you is holy, you also be holy in all your conduct [*anastrophē*], since it is written, "You shall be holy, for I am holy." And if you call on him as Father who judges impartially according to each one's deeds [*ergon*], conduct yourselves [*anastrophēte*] with fear throughout the time of your exile, knowing that you were ransomed from the futile ways [*anastrophēs*] inherited from your forefathers, not with perishable things such as silver or gold, but with the precious blood of Christ, like that of a lamb without blemish or spot.

Like Paul, Peter contrasts a former way of life with that of a new behavior. Howe asserts of Peter's use of *anastrophē*, "The word 'behavior,' which translates ἀναστροφή, corresponds to the word 'lifestyle' and covers all actions, thoughts, words, and relationships."[21] Peter characterizes the former behavior as flowing from ignorance, leading to "futile ways inherited

---

20. Frank E. Gaebelein, gen. ed., *The Expositor's Bible Commentary, Volume 11: Ephesians through Philemon* (Grand Rapids: Zondervan Publishing House, 1981), 62.
21. Frederic R. Howe, "The Christian Life in Peter's Theology," *Bibliotheca Sacra* 157, no. 627 (July 2000): 306–7.

from your forefathers." The new way is to be characterized by holiness and fear. Here Peter uses the verb form of *anastrophē, anastrephō*, to command his readers to live a certain way since they have been ransomed from the former life. Peter also uses a nearly synonymous "behavior"-related term, *ergon* ("deeds"), to describe their lifestyle.

Later in 1 Peter 2:12 Peter admonishes his readers, "Keep your conduct [*anastrophēn*] among the Gentiles [*ethnesin*] honorable, so that when they speak against you as evildoers, they may see your good deeds [*ergon*] and glorify God on the day of visitation." Notably, this command is in the context of Peter using terms related to ethnicity to call believers in Christ a "chosen race [*genos*]," "a holy nation [*ethnos*]," and "a people [*laos*] for his own possession." This, then, reveals a connection between the terms related to ethnicity and those related to behavior. *Genos, ethnos*, and *laos* identify groups of people who unite around common *anastrophē*. This common behavior stems from shared values and beliefs. Christians, according to Peter, are members of a new race who possess common values and beliefs that result in a new way of life. This pattern of conduct is distinct from their former behavior, the conduct of unbelievers. Indeed, the metaphorical use of *ethnos* in several passages, including 1 Peter 2:9, indicates that the Christian community forms a new "nation" distinct from earthly nations. David Wright explains the significance of the terms related to ethnic identity in 1 Peter 2:

> Each of these four designations is pregnant with suggestiveness of its own, but they all express the important early Christian conviction that Christians in any one place or region belonged to a people, the people of God, which constituted a new corporate presence. This self-consciousness became a significant feature of the remarkable confidence of the Christians in the first three centuries.[22]

Wright argues that the early church saw itself as a "third race," distinct from other earthly races, and thus it rejected the behavior of those races. Christians are a new race, not because they happen to choose a new way

---

22. David F. Wright, "A Race Apart? Jews, Gentiles, Christians," *Bibliotheca Sacra* 160, no. 368 (April 2003): 128.

of life; rather, they have a new spiritual genetic heritage that produces a distinct conduct.

First Peter 2:12 also reveals another important aspect of a believer's conduct—it has potential evangelistic impact upon unbelievers: "They may see your good deeds and glorify God on the day of visitation." Peter reiterates this emphasis in 1 Peter 3:1–2: "Likewise, wives, be subject to your own husbands, so that even if some do not obey the word, they may be won without a word by the conduct [*anastrophēs*] of their wives, when they see your respectful and pure conduct [*anastrophēn*]." Also important to note is that Peter describes this "pure conduct" in terms of particular ways of adorning themselves in jewelry and dress, i.e., "cultural" products (vv 3–6). Finally, Peter further describes the importance of a believer's way of life for its significance in evangelism in 1 Peter 3:15–16:

> But in your hearts honor Christ the Lord as holy, always being prepared to make a defense to anyone who asks you for a reason for the hope that is in you; yet do it with gentleness and respect, having a good conscience, so that, when you are slandered, those who revile your good behavior [*anastrophēn*] in Christ may be put to shame.

A New Testament Understanding of Culture

This study reveals that the New Testament terms most closely resembling both cultural anthropologists' and missional authors' definitions of "culture" are those related to behavior. While both the terms related to ethnic identity and those related to "the world" demonstrate relationship to the contemporary notion of culture, they do not identify culture itself. Ethnic groups unite around common culture, and the sinful world-system affects unbelieving culture, but these terms are not the same as culture. Rather, behavior-related terms like *anastrophē*—which describe complete ways of life, conduct, and behavior—most closely identify "that complex whole which includes knowledge, belief, arts, morals, law, custom, and any other capabilities and habits acquired by man as a member of society" (Tylor)[23] or "the sum total of ways of living

---

23. Tylor, *Primitive Culture*, 1.

built up by a human community and transmitted from one generation to another" (Newbigin).[24]

If there is any concept of the anthropological/missional idea of "culture" in the New Testament, it is the idea of "way of life." A people's culture is their behavior and their conduct. Several important implications may be drawn from this analysis. First, New Testament authors explain cultural differences between various people groups as differences of belief and value. They highlight differences of belief and religion that produce the behavior and conduct of a people. This is important because it contradicts the idea of cultural neutrality. Since values and beliefs are not neutral (i.e., they are either good or evil), the culture produced from values and beliefs is likewise not neutral. Furthermore, this also contradicts the notion that religion is a component of culture. Rather, culture is a component of religion. So while "behavior"-related terms resemble anthropological/missional definitions of culture, the use of such terms in the New Testament should reorient the missional understanding of culture such that it is seen as flowing from religious values and worldview. Thus every culture and particular cultural expression must be evaluated based upon what religious values it embodies.

Second, New Testament authors identify people groups (ethnicities, tribes, nations, etc.) as those of common ancestral heritage who share common culture flowing from common values. They do not think about "culture" as such; rather, they think about behavior, and they believe that the gospel changes behavior—it changes a person's culture. Since culture is a component of religion, where religion changes, so changes culture. This creates a reorientation of race for Christians; since a race is a group that shares common values and practices, Christians will find themselves increasingly alienated from the race into which they were born and drawn into a new race united around biblical values.

Third, New Testament authors demand that the culture of Christians be holy, pure, and distinct from the culture of unbelievers. Rather than understanding culture to be neutral, New Testament authors judge unbelieving culture as worthy of condemnation. They expect Christians, therefore, to reject the culture shaped by the world's systems and to form a new way of life impacted by biblical values. The culture produced from

---

24. Newbigin, *The Other Side of 1984*, 5.

unbelief is not neutral; it is depraved. As Snoeberger notes, "Cultural neutrality is a myth and culture is hostile toward God; just as man is individually depraved in microcosm, so also culture is corporately depraved in macrocosm."[25]

Fourth, New Testament authors proclaim Christianity as a new and distinct people group that shares new values and thus new culture. Peter in particular identifies Christians as a "chosen race," a "holy nation," and a "people for [God's] own possession" distinct from other races, nations, and peoples. Howe summarizes the important relationship between terms related to ethnicity and behavior in Peter's writing:

> The word *anastrophēs*, "way of life," is a key word in Petrine theology, for it occurs eight times in Peter's epistles (1 Peter 1:15, 18; 2:12; 3:1, 2, 16; 2 Peter 2:7; 3:11). The contrast of lifestyles of believers before and after they trusted Christ as their Redeemer is vividly displayed by seeing how the same word is used to describe their former way of life ("your futile way of life [*anastrophēs*]," 1:18) and their new life in Christ ("be holy yourselves also in all your behavior [*anastrophē*]," 1:15).
>
> This contrast serves as evidence that Peter sought to relate the theological significance of the death of Christ to the ethical dimension of the lives of those who trusted his finished work for their salvation.[26]

Fifth, New Testament authors insist that a clear distinction between the culture of believers and unbelievers will have evangelistic impact. Missional authors, however, argue that in order to reach the culture, believers must be incarnate in the culture, that is, they must resemble the culture around them. Unbelievers will be evangelized only as they recognize the presentation of the gospel in their own cultural language. The advocacy of contextualization by missional authors flows directly from their understanding of culture as something entirely involuntary and neutral. Evangelism cannot occur, they argue, without cultural contextualization.

---

25. Snoeberger, "Noetic Sin, Neutrality, and Contextualization," 357.
26. Howe, "The Christian Life in Peter's Theology," 194.

While this is certainly true with regard to language intelligibility, mission-al authors extend "intelligibility" to all aspects of behavior. In contrast, New Testament authors insist that only when the culture of believers changes as a result of transformed values will unbelievers "glorify God on the day of visitation." Snoeberger explains this more biblical approach to evangelizing the culture: "The proper response of the Christian to culture is to expose its depravity, demonstrate that it has illicitly borrowed from the Christian worldview, and show that its adherents cannot live within the implications of their own worldview."[27]

Snoeberger's comments lead to one final conclusion that must be drawn as a result of synthesizing what the New Testament authors reveal about pagan and Christian culture: where similarities do exist between the behavior of unbelievers and the conduct of believers, such behavior by unbelievers is due to the fact that on that particular issue they are working with what Greg Bahnsen calls "borrowed capital"[28]—unbelievers borrow-ing biblical values in certain areas of their lives. Snoeberger explains:

> Some cultures borrow substantially from the Christian world-view (sometimes consciously and deliberately, but more often in subconscious response to the latent influence of common grace that envelopes all of God's creation) and others do not, and this factor is singularly vital in determining how a Chris-tian is to relate to culture.[29]

This reality explains why the culture of Christians may at times resem-ble the culture of unbelievers in some respects. However, this under-standing also sets the believer's initial response toward an unbelieving culture as one of suspicion until he can determine which aspects reveal a borrowing from biblical values. Furthermore, when certain aspects of an unbelieving culture and a biblical culture resemble one another, it is because the unbelievers look like Christians in those instances, not the other way around.

---

27. Snoeberger, "Noetic Sin, Neutrality, and Contextualization," 357.
28. Greg L. Bahnsen, *Pushing the Antithesis: The Apologetic Methodology of Greg L. Bahnsen* (Pow-der Springs, GA: American Vision, 2007), 103.
29. Mark A. Snoeberger, "D. A. Carson's Christ and Culture Revisited: A Reflection and a Re-sponse," *Detroit Baptist Seminary Journal* 13 (2008): 100.

Christians in the twenty-first century will not be able to escape wrestling through matters of culture and contextualization as they seek to accomplish the mission God has for them. Yet rather than adopting the understanding of culture developed by secular anthropologists, Christians should be willing to reorient that viewpoint to fit within the biblical categories of behavior and conduct, applying all that the Scripture has to offer about those categories to cultural matters. Only then will they be equipped to appropriate a truly biblical perspective on culture and contextualization for world evangelism, worship, and the entirety of church ministry.

chapter 7

LANGUAGE, LITERATURE, AND THE KING'S MEAT: A BIBLICAL MODEL FOR CULTURAL ENGAGEMENT

Then the king commanded Ashpenaz . . .
to bring some of the people of Israel . . .
and to teach them the literature and language of the Chaldeans. . . .
But Daniel resolved that he would not defile himself with the king's food,
or with the wine that he drank.
Daniel 1:3–4, 8

One of the clearest examples from Israel's time in Babylonian captivity of a kind of discerning contextualization that I am advocating is found in Daniel 1. Here Daniel both embraces some aspects of Babylonian culture (their "literature and language"), yet he rejects other aspects ("the king's food"). He did not simply accept uncritically all of their culture, but neither did he reject it all either. This kind of critical evaluation of culture is more fitting with a biblical understanding of the nature of culture presented in the last chapter, and reflects the New Testament's emphasis as well.

"Contextualization" in the New Testament

As noted above, the missional philosophy of contextualization depends heavily upon adaption of the anthropological definition of culture. Thus defining culture biblically as "behavior" or "way of life" already reorients the idea of contextualization. However, a brief analysis of the key passages cited as examples of biblical contextualization will further clarify whether such comparisons are valid. Missional proponents identify two passages primarily as examples of New Testament contextualization.

Mars Hill
Chapter 2 revealed several cases in which missional authors cite Acts 17:16–34 as a model for missional contextualization. An examination of this passage demonstrates weaknesses in typical missional applications of this passage, however, especially to corporate worship.

Acts 17 records Paul's attempt to evangelize three cities, each of which had very different kinds of people. Paul's audience in Thessalonica was predominantly Jewish. He spent time in the synagogue there speaking to Jews and Jewish proselytes, but it was not a receptive audience. Some did come to Christ, but for the most part, Paul's audience was hostile. Verse 5 records that these Jews were jealous when a few began to convert to Christ, and so they stirred up the crowd against Paul. In Paul's first letter to the Thessalonians he notes that they received the gospel amid affliction (1:6). In his second letter he reminded them that they accepted his message in the midst of much conflict (2:2). So evidently the few who did come to Christ did so despite much persecution.

In Berea, Paul's audience was mostly Jewish, but these Jews were generally open to his message. Verse 11 states that they were more noble than the Thessalonians because they received Paul's message with eagerness, so this audience was similar to the one in Thessalonica except that they were much more receptive.

After Berea, Paul went to Athens, where his audience was much different than the other two cities. Athens was the center of Greek mythology, which in verse 16 Paul noticed when he saw that the city was full of idols.[1] Furthermore, this city contained a number of high class philosophers, exemplified by whom Paul meets in verse 18, a group of Epicureans and Stoics. Epicureans were pure materialists who did not believe in the spiritual world, similar to secular humanists today. Stoics were pantheists. Not only did they believe in many gods, but they also believed that all people have divinity within them, similar to modern New Age beliefs.[2] So this was a completely different kind of audience than those that Paul had found in Thessalonica and Berea.

Thus Acts 17 records Paul's attempt to communicate the gospel to these three different audiences. The question is whether Paul contextualized the message depending on the culture he was in, and if so, to what degree. Verse 2 records that he reasoned with the Jews in Thessalonica from the Old Testament Scriptures. These Jews would have respected the Scriptures as inspired by God, and so it was natural for Paul to start there. Verse 3 records that he explained those Scriptures to them and proved that the Messiah had to die and rise again, and then he explained to them that the facts about Jesus of Nazareth fulfilled these prophesies about the Messiah. The proper response would be to believe in Jesus Christ. Paul could make assumptions with these Jews, he could leave some things unsaid, and he reasoned from Old Testament prophecies. His method was evidently similar with the Berean Jews.

Paul's method differed with the audience in Athens, which needed more information than the Jews. He had to tell them that God created all things and ruled them all, that God expected them to serve him, and that judgment was coming for those who did not. The Jews already believed this, but he had to explain these issues to the Athenians because, as he said, they were ignorant. In Athens, Paul did not reason with them out of messianic prophesies, trying to prove that predictions about the Messiah and facts about Jesus's life matched, which would have made no sense to them. Instead, he appealed to the needs he knew the Athenians had and showed them why they needed to turn to God.

In this sense, Paul presented the same gospel message in different ways depending on his audience. The first way Paul communicated differently was in relation to their religion. With the Jews in Thessalonica and Berea, Paul was able to build on the foundation of their current religion and explain

---

1. Mal Couch, *A Bible Handbook to the Acts of the Apostles* (Grand Rapids: Kregel Academic, 2004), 338–39.
2. John B. Polhill, *Acts* (Nashville: B&H Publishing Group, 1992), 336–37.

new revelation concerning Jesus. He could not do that with pagans since they had a different understanding of the nature of the world, and so Paul had to consider their current religious understanding and then explain what was necessary to correct their faulty thinking. He does this in verses 22–23:

> So Paul, standing in the midst of the Areopagus, said: "Men of Athens, I perceive that in every way you are very religious. For as I passed along and observed the objects of your worship, I found also an altar with this inscription, 'To the unknown god.' What therefore you worship as unknown, this I proclaim to you."

Paul had evidently spent some time studying the religion of Athens, and he used that knowledge to present the gospel in the best way possible, but what Paul thought about this religious culture is enlightening. Verse 16 reveals that Paul was "provoked" (*parōxyneto*) by the culture he saw in Athens.[3] He did not adopt their culture; he did not approve of their culture; he despised it. Furthermore, Paul did not try to garner respect by speaking positively about their beliefs. In verse 22, when he says that they are "religious," he is not complimenting them. The word here is *deisidaimōn*, literally "superstitious," which would have been considered a negative charge.[4] Although some might suggest that the term is neutral, Paul's other use in Romans 1:20–23 is a decidedly negative tone and communicates spiritual ignorance.[5] This is reflected further in verse 23 where Paul references their "unknown" god. Again, some missional advocates suggest that Paul was seeking to gain common ground with his audience.[6] However, Paul's use of the term *agnoeō* here again connotes a negative charge of ignorance. The NASB is perhaps the clearest translation here: "What therefore you worship in ignorance, this I proclaim to you."[7] Even the phrase "objects of your worship" is used elsewhere in Scripture only negatively.[8] Thus Paul was accusing his audience of

---

3. Cf. John R. W. Stott, *The Message of Acts: The Spirit, the Church, and the World* (Bible Speaks Today), reprint (Downers Grove, IL: InterVarsity Press, 1994), 278.
4. David Peterson, *The Acts of the Apostles* (Grand Rapids: Wm. B. Eerdmans, 2009), 494. Cf. Polhill, *Acts*, 371.
5. Darrell L. Bock, *Acts* (Grand Rapids: Baker Academic, 2007), 564.
6. Lynn Allan Losie, "Paul's Speech on the Areopagus: A Model of Cross-Cultural Evangelism," in *Mission in Acts: Ancient Narratives in Contemporary Context*, ed. Robert L. Gallagher and Paul Hertig (Maryknoll, NY: Orbis Books, 2004), 229–30.
7. Polhill, *Acts*, 372; R. Kent Hughes, *Acts: The Church Afire* (Wheaton, IL: Crossway, 1996), 233.
8. Cf. 2 Thessalonians 2:4 and Romans 1:25.

being ignorant in their religious beliefs. In fact, he implies their ignorance again in verse 30 and says that God commands them to repent of it.

Paul continues by addressing their philosophy. In verse 28, Paul quotes their own philosophers: "For 'In him we live and move and have our being'; as even some of your own poets have said, 'For we are indeed his offspring.'" Some might insist that this is an example of Paul immersing himself in the culture of Athens and quoting their own philosophers as a way to gain respect from his audience. However, careful consideration of Paul's argument here clarifies the issue. His primary argument begins in verse 24:

> The God who made the world and everything in it, being Lord of heaven and earth, does not live in temples made by man, nor is he served by human hands, as though he needed anything, since he himself gives to all mankind life and breath and everything. And he made from one man every nation of mankind to live on all the face of the earth, having determined allotted periods and the boundaries of their dwelling place, that they should seek God, and perhaps feel their way toward him and find him. Yet he is actually not far from each one of us.

Paul's argument is that God is the Creator and Ruler of all and that he is not served by human hands. Then he quotes their own philosophers who admit that they come from a god, which reveals their inconsistency. They say that they came from a god, and yet they still try to bring that god under their control by making idols. Paul is attempting to discredit them by pointing out this glaring inconsistency in their thinking. He reveals that purpose in verse 29:

> Being then God's offspring, we ought not to think that the divine being is like gold or silver or stone, an image formed by the art and imagination of man.

Paul was not using cultural references in a positive light; again, he was showing how futile they were. He was discrediting the popular religious philosophy of the day.

Paul did communicate the message of the gospel differently to pagans than he did to Jews. However, the difference involved the fact that he could build on the truth of the Jewish religion, while his attitude toward the religion of the pagans was one of disgust and condemnation. He did not immerse himself in their "culture" in order to reach them; instead, he exploited the ignorance and superstition of their religion in order to confront them with the truths of the gospel. Rather than highlighting similarities between his worldview and that of the Athenians and seeking to express the gospel in their philosophical categories, as missional authors suggest, Paul was pressing the antithesis between their worldviews and ways of life in order to reveal the inconsistencies in their own thinking and highlight the authority of the Christian worldview.

All Things to All Men

Missional experts also appeal to 1 Corinthians 9:19–23 as an example of cultural contextualization:

> For though I am free from all, I have made myself a servant to all, that I might win more of them. To the Jews I became as a Jew, in order to win Jews. To those under the law I became as one under the law (though not being myself under the law) that I might win those under the law. To those outside the law I became as one outside the law (not being outside the law of God but under the law of Christ) that I might win those outside the law. To the weak I became weak, that I might win the weak. I have become all things to all people, that by all means I might save some. I do it all for the sake of the gospel, that I may share with them in its blessings.

Missional authors use this passage to support the position that churches must be willing to change any aspect of their ministry for the sake of the gospel. This philosophy is at the root of desires to change worship style, for example, and provides the basis for Stetzer's assertion that worship must not be "constrained by the values and vision of supporters who are already Christ followers."[9]

In order to discern the central message of this passage, it must be understood in its larger context of a discussion about meat that had been offered to idols in 1 Corinthians 8–10. Paul argues in chapter 8 that the

---

9. Stetzer, *Planting Missional Churches*, 267.

meat itself is good, but for several reasons expounded in the subsequent chapters, Paul suggests that in some circumstances Christians may be wisest to refrain from eating. If the meat is so strongly identified with the idol worship that it causes weaker Christians to stumble into sin, then the stronger Christian should not eat the meat (8:13). In chapter 9, Paul reinforces his point by listing other rights that he would be willing to forego for the sake of the gospel. For Paul, unhindered communication of the gospel motivates him to forsake what are legitimately his rights (9:18).

In this context, Paul makes his famous "all things to all men" statement. Missional advocates understand this to be a positive statement of adopting the culture of a target audience in order to reach them for the gospel. However, the context of the argument proves differently. Paul is not suggesting that the evangelist adopt cultural practices in order to engage his audience; rather, he is insisting that the evangelist be willing to eliminate practices that may be within his rights if such practices will hinder the advancement of the gospel. This is John Makujina's argument. "Contextualization" in this sense, according to Makujina, should be "preventative and defensive" rather than "offensive." Paul is not attempting to create a "persuasive advantage with his hearers when the gospel is presented"; rather, he removes barriers to the gospel in order to create a "zero, neutral ground from which he may preach Christ crucified."[10] Wilder summarizes:

> Paul willingly gave up the exercise of his rights "on account of the gospel" and by doing so saw himself as participating in it (9:23).... For the sake of Christian love and the propagation of the gospel of Christ, we need to be willing to refrain from the exercise of any rights that we may have as believers or individuals.[11]

Even if the missional philosophy of contextualization is based on an anthropological understanding of culture, their idea of contextualization cannot be proven from the passages discussed above. Adjusting methods of communicating the gospel based on religious differences or removing legitimate practices that would hinder the gospel are not the same as the

---

10. John Makujina, *Measuring the Music: Another Look at the Contemporary Christian Music Debate* (Willow Street, PA: Old Paths Publications, 2002), 20–23.
11. Terry L. Wilder, "A Biblical Theology of Mission and Contextualization," *Southwestern Journal of Theology* 55, no. 1 (Fall 2012): 16–17.

contemporary evangelical notion of contextualization that involves immersing one's self in the cultural practices of a target audience in order to gain a hearing for the gospel.

A New Testament Approach to Christ and Culture

The survey of contemporary understandings of culture and contextualization in the last chapter followed by an exposition of related biblical ideas in this chapter reveal a more scriptural framework through which to approach cultural issues today. Niebuhr's classic categories (chapter 4, pp. 55–56) have often been critiqued for the fact that few people fit neatly into any one of them, and for good reason. As the survey in chapter 4 illustrates, there is much in common among the typical approaches as well as considerable overlap. Furthermore, Niebuhr has also been criticized on the grounds that he considers culture as something monolithic, a charge that could as equally apply to the approaches evaluated above. D. A. Carson helpfully summarizes the apparent problem one faces when evaluating the popular approaches to culture:

> What this potted survey ought to tell us is that none of the powerfully advanced theories commonly put forward to explain the relationships between Christ and culture or to implement an improved dynamic is very compelling as a total explanation or an unambiguous mandate. Each has decided strengths; some are better at drawing in the highly diverse and complementary strands of Scripture and historical interpretation than others whose coinage is reductionism. Moreover, as empirically useful as certain grids may be, thoughtful Christians need to adopt an extra degree of hesitation about canonizing any of them in an age in which we are learning the extent to which our own cultural locations contributes, for better and for worse, to our understanding of these theological matters, as of all theological matters.[12]

Carson's solution is to argue that the Christian will have to adopt both stances toward culture depending on the situation:

---

12. Carson, *Christ and Culture Revisited*, 224.

Instead of imagining that Christ *against* culture and Christ *transforming* culture are two mutually exclusive stances, the rich complexity of biblical norms, worked out in the Bible's story line, tells us that these two often operate simultaneously.[13]

Andy Crouch treats the issue similarly. He suggests that each of the approaches is appropriate in certain circumstances and not in others; none of the approaches, he argues, should be adopted in all circumstances. He uses the terms *postures* and *gestures* to differentiate between the two. The various approaches to culture should never become a *posture*—an "unconscious default position"; rather we may adopt a given approach as a *gesture* depending on the nature of the situation. He summarizes:

> Indeed, the appeal of the various postures of condemning, critiquing, copying and consuming—the reason that all of them are still very much with us—is that each of these responses to culture is, at certain times and with specific cultural goods, a necessary gesture.[14]

The problem with each of these evaluations of cultural engagement, however, is rooted in ambiguity regarding the nature of culture itself. Niebuhr and some advocates of the approaches evaluated above seem to see it as something monolithic—more of a Christendom idea of culture. Others see it as entirely neutral, the use (or "direction") of cultural artifacts being the only legitimate grounds for judgment. Therefore, an explicitly biblical understanding of culture as expressed in this chapter is necessary in order to discern the most biblical approach to culture and contextualization.

"Culture" as Behavior

I have argued that the closest approximation to the contemporary understanding of culture in Scripture is "behavior," expressed most clearly by terms such as *anastrophē*. This understanding has several benefits for the discussion at hand. First, culture is not monolithic but consists of various behaviors and ways of living that differ among in-

---

13. Ibid., 227. Emphasis original.
14. Crouch, *Culture Making*, 90.

dividuals and civilizations. Second, culture is not neutral but involves ways of acting out values. Third, application of this understanding of culture as behavior will give much clearer direction concerning how a Christian should respond with regard to his own behavior and the behavior (i.e., "culture") of unbelievers.

Application of the New Testament to Culture as Behavior

If the idea of "culture" in the New Testament is essentially "behavior," then the biblical approach to culture becomes more apparent. From the New Testament discussions of *anastrophē*, several important realities emerge.

First, unholy culture exists. The Bible is clear that mankind, left to himself, is utterly corrupt. Even though God created all things good and even manifests himself generally in that creation (Ps. 19:1–2), mankind continually rejects him and is therefore under God's condemnation (Rom. 1:18–32). Mankind not only refuses God's revelation, it *cannot* accept God on its own (1 Cor. 2:14).

Disagreement over whether mankind is entirely corrupt was at the heart of debates between the Roman Church and the Reformers.[15] The Christendom, Christ-above-culture model believed that the church and society could be fused based on the assumption that there was an inherent goodness present even among unbelievers. Each of the post-Christendom approaches to culture, however, rejected this perspective on the basis of the doctrine of antithesis: depravity creates a strict division between the values of Christians and unbelievers.

Sinful culture exists because culture, understood as behavior, is a reflection of values. The apostle Paul speaks of his former sinful culture when he says, "For you have heard of my former life (*anastrophēn*) in Judaism, how I persecuted the church of God violently and tried to destroy it" (Gal. 1:13). His was a culture of hatred and violence toward the true people of God. Furthermore, Peter speaks of "the sensual conduct (*anastrophēs*) of the wicked" (2 Peter 2:7) and "those who live (*anastrophomenous*) in error" (2 Peter 2:18). Particular behaviors are

---

15. See Martin Luther and Desiderius Erasmus, *Luther and Erasmus: Free Will and Salvation*, ed. E. Gordon Rupp and Philip S. Watson (Philadelphia: Westminster John Knox Press, 1969).

sinful when they are expressions of sinful values. The values of Judaism ran contrary to the values of Christianity, and therefore it was Paul's culture to persecute Christians. The values of wickedness lead to a certain kind of sensual culture.

The transformationalists are correct when they identify worldview as the center of antithesis between good and evil, but they are incorrect to insist that culture is neutral. Worldview and culture are inextricably linked. One's behavior is an expression of his values; sinful values produce sinful behavior. Therefore an antithesis between the culture of believers and unbelievers exists when unbelievers' behavior reflects sinful values.

Second, Christians are redeemed from unholy culture. Paul states that even believers "once lived (*anastrophēn*) in the passions of [their] flesh" (Eph. 2:3), but through Christ, God has raised believers out of such unholy behavior (vv. 5–6). This is why Paul commands Christians later in Ephesians 4:22 to "put off your old self, which belongs to your former manner of life (*anastrophēv*)." Believers are to reject actively the sinful behavior that flows from sinful values expressly because they are "ransomed from the futile ways (*anastrophēs*)" (1 Peter 1:18). Contrary to transformationalists, the "futile ways" themselves are not redeemed; *individuals* are redeemed *away from* such sinful culture. Behavior that flows from sinful values is irredeemable just as the values themselves are irredeemable. True, redemption results in transformation, but this transformation results in entirely different culture than the "former manner of life."

As discussed above, when transformationalists talk about "transformation of culture," they refer only to the content of cultural artifacts rather than the artifacts themselves. They affirm an antithesis between worldviews, but they deny such an antithesis exists in cultural expressions themselves. For the transformationalist, only the content of culture expresses worldview, not cultural forms. Understanding culture as behavior destroys this notion. It is not simply the content of cultural artifacts that expresses worldview as the transformationalists argue, but rather it is the cultural artifact itself that expresses certain values. Thus if the value that produces the artifact is unholy, the artifact itself is also unholy. The transformationalists commit a category error by essentially equating culture with creation and content with value. Rather, both the content and the cultural vehicle express values.

Third, a fundamental antithesis exists between the values of Christians and unbelievers, but not always between their behaviors. Up to this point, antithesis has been emphasized to the degree that the separatism of the Radical Reformers may seem the most biblical approach to the culture of unbelievers. If culture is an expression of worldview, and if there exists a fundamental antithesis between the worldview of believers and unbelievers, then certainly Christians can have no commonality with the culture of unbelievers.

However, two additional biblical realities alter the picture. First, the transformationalists are correct in that God gives a certain measure of common grace to all people. God's common grace enables even unbelievers to possess certain biblical values and thus behave in biblical ways. The classic definition of common grace comes from John Murray: "every favor of whatever kind or degree, falling short of salvation, which the undeserving and sin-cursed world enjoys at the hand of God."[16] Matthew 5:44–45 and Luke 6:35 relate God's favor to unbelievers in this way. Common grace enables unbelievers to maintain relatively peaceful and successful civilizations. In fact, the institution of government itself is an act of grace from God.

The reality of common grace leads to another recognition, the fact that unbelievers can indeed behave in biblical ways. Jesus himself said that sinners can do good (Luke 6:33). This is perhaps explained through the two-kingdom doctrine of natural law, expressed in passages like Romans 2:14–15:

> For when Gentiles, who do not have the law, by nature do (*poiōsin*) what the law requires, they are a law to themselves, even though they do not have the law. They show that the work of the law is written on their hearts, while their conscience also bears witness, and their conflicting thoughts accuse or even excuse them.

This passage uses another "behavior"-related term, *poieō* ("do") and expresses that even Gentile unbelievers can "do what the law requires" since

---

16. John Murray, "Common Grace," in *Collected Writings of John Murray*, vol. 2 (Carlisle, PA: Banner of Truth, 1991), 96.

"the law is written on their hearts." This may reflect the two-kingdom's "natural law," or it may be what transformationalist Greg Bahnsen calls "borrowed capital"—unbelievers borrowing biblical values in certain areas of their lives. Either way, Scripture is clear that sometimes the behavior of unbelievers is good, and thus in such cases commonality can exist between the culture of believers and unbelievers.

Fourth, holy values ought to affect every aspect of a Christian's behavior. The Bible is clear with regard to the behavior of Christians—it is to be holy. James states of a Christian, "by his good conduct (*anastrophēs*) let him show his works" (James 3:13). Likewise Peter commands Christians to "be holy in all [their] conduct (*anastrophē*)" (1 Peter 1:15), and Paul commands Timothy to set an example "in conduct (*anastrophē*)" (1 Tim. 4:12). These commands do not apply only in "sacred" things, but in all of life. A Christian is a new creation with new values (2 Cor. 5:17), and those values will affect every aspect of his culture. For example, after commanding believers to put off the "old self, which belongs to [their] former [culture]" (Eph. 4:22), Paul details several different areas in which the new self will manifest itself, including relationships with neighbors (v. 25), work ethic (v. 28), and communication (v. 29). The outcome of new values is new culture in every aspect of life.

Thus, Kuyper may have been correct when he talked about distinctly Christian approaches to the various spheres of life. His most famous statement is certainly true when understanding culture as behavior: "There is not a square inch in the whole domain of our human existence over which Christ, who is Sovereign over *all*, does not cry: 'Mine!'" Christian values will produce carpentry, justice, rhetoric, and music that are influenced by their Christian values, although even unbelievers can do the same because of common grace and if they borrow from the Christian worldview. Perhaps VanDrunen is right that calling such things "Christian" is misleading, but the underlying sentiment is scriptural: any behavior that is an expression of biblical values can rightly be called "biblical." If "Christian" is not the best adjective for reasons raised by VanDrunen, perhaps "holy" best reflects the Bible's admonitions.

Fifth, the Word of God alone governs the behavior of the church as an institution. The danger VanDrunen expressed regarding describing behaviors in the civic sphere as "Christian" is that when everything becomes Christian, nothing is Christian. In this concern he is right, especially in evaluating the transformationalists' ecclesiology. For the transformationalist, there is essentially no difference between what happens in the church as an institution and what a Christian does—all of life is worship. This is especially true for the missional church movement. Seeking to escape "ecclesiocentrism," missional advocates subsume the mission of the church under the *missio Dei*, and thus the mission of the church and the mission of individual Christians are the same.

Yet the biblical picture is different. All of life may be worship in its broadest sense, but the worship of the corporate church is distinct from the worship of individual Christians in their everyday lives. The New Testament refers to the behavior of the church as an institution distinct from, although certainly related to, that of an individual Christian. For example, Paul writes to Timothy so that he "may know how to behave (*anastrophesthai*) in the household of God, which is the church of the living God, a pillar and buttress of the truth" (1 Tim. 3:15). Behavior within the household of God is to be governed by express prescriptions from the Word of God alone. The individual Christian's life, on the other hand, while certainly guided by Scripture and affected by biblical values, nevertheless operates more broadly. This in itself demonstrates a distinction between the government of the church and the civic government.

Sixth, the relationship between holy culture and unholy culture should be one of witness. The separatist sees the relationship between the church and "unholy" culture as one of complete separation. Two-kingdom advocates also see the two as completely distinct but encourage Christians to involve themselves in the civic realm for the good of mankind. Transformationalists see the relationship as one of redemption and kingdom-building, blurring any real distinction between the two.

Understanding "culture" to be "behavior," the biblical picture appears to be somewhat different from all three, although overlapping in some areas. As explained above, the Bible does recognize a separation between the behavior of believers and unbelievers when the unbeliever's behavior is unholy. Yet this separation itself is what has evangelistic impact. Peter admonishes believers to "keep your conduct (*anastrophēn*) among the Gentiles honorable" so that "they may see your good deeds (*ergōn*) and glorify

God on the day of visitation" (1 Peter 2:12). He tells women that their unbelieving husbands "may be won by [their] conduct (*anastrophēs*)" (1 Peter 3:1–2). Contrary to the missional transformationalists, unbelievers will not be won by adopting or adapting ("transforming") their unholy culture. Rather, expressing holy values through holy culture will reveal the deficiencies in the values and behaviors of the unbelievers, which may have a convicting influence and lead them to Christ.

Seventh, only holy culture will remain. Again, contrary to transformationalists, who argue that they are transforming culture in such a way that it will remain in the eschaton, and missionalists, who insist that all the cultures of the world will remain in heaven, the New Testament is clear that only holy culture will remain; all else will pass away: "Since all these things are thus to be dissolved, what sort of people ought you to be in lives (*anastrophais*) of holiness and godliness" (2 Peter 3:11). Of course, this fact is built on all of the previous discussion; if only holy values will remain, and culture is the expression of values, then only holy culture will remain in the end.

The Sanctificationist Approach to Culture

What is clear from this exploration is that each of the three primary post-Christendom approaches to culture has strengths and weaknesses when compared to the New Testament's understanding of culture as behavior. The separatist approach rightly recognizes the fundamental antithesis between belief and unbelief, but it fails to also recognize commonality that exists due to common grace and the fact that even unbelievers sometimes "borrow" a biblical worldview. The transformationalist approach rightly recognizes the reality of common grace on the cultures of unbelievers and the need for Christians to express their values in every sphere of life, but they do so to the neglect of any real antithesis in the cultures themselves. Perhaps the two-kingdom approach is closest to the New Testament perspective, with its balance of both antithesis and commonality, but it fails to emphasize that a Christian's involvement in the culture should manifest his Christian values and actually has evangelistic impact.

Understanding culture as behavior provides a fourth alternative that combines the strengths of each view and protects against their respective weaknesses. This view, which could be called the sanctificationist approach to culture, simply seeks to apply what the Bible has to say about behavior to every area of the Christian's life. A Christian is to be holy in all of his conduct; the Holy Spirit uses the Bible to progressively sanctify that conduct each day. A Christian does not have to overly concern himself with whether or not he may adopt the behavior of others; he simply lives out his Christian life according to the precepts found in Scripture. When the behavior of unbelievers reflects those same precepts, he will resemble the unbeliever's culture; when it does not, separation must take place. Nevertheless, in either case, the believer's good conduct among the unbelievers will shine forth as a beacon of truth to draw them to redemption in Jesus Christ. And when they are redeemed, their culture will change. Perhaps the best New Testament posture for Christians who are in the world but not of the world is found in 1 Peter 1:17–18:

> And if you call on him as Father who judges impartially according to each one's deeds (*ergon*), conduct yourselves (*anastrophēte*) with fear throughout the time of your exile, knowing that you were ransomed from the futile ways (*anastrophēs*) inherited from your forefathers.

chapter 8

FUTURE HOPE: WORSHIP IN

THE HEAVENLY JERUSALEM

How lovely is your dwelling place,
O LORD of hosts!
My soul longs, yes, faints
for the courts of the LORD;
my heart and flesh sing for joy
to the living God.
Psalm 84:1–2

The Israelites wept while they remained in captivity because they could not sing the songs that rightfully belonged in their Temple in their land. Today, Christians do not weep over their captivity; instead, they sing the songs of their captives!

Yet neither alternative is right for the Christian. We need not withdraw ourselves in cloisters and refuse to worship because we find ourselves in a strange land. Neither should we welcome in the songs of the pagans, even with noble motives of reaching them with our message of good news.

Rather, the New Testament understanding of culture and contextualization presented in the previous chapter provides a framework for articulating an alternative philosophy of corporate worship in a post-Christian culture, especially in the context of desiring to reach people in that culture with the gospel of Jesus Christ. The purpose of this chapter is to establish a biblical understanding of distinctly Christian worship, an understanding that recognizes that although we are currently in captivity, we need not long for a Temple far off in a distant land; as Christians, we are welcomed into the heavenly Jerusalem through Christ.

Drawing Near to God

In order to grasp the essence of Christian worship, we must start in the beginning. Creation provides the foundation for understanding not only the nature of God and mankind but also the substance of their relationship in worship. God, the sovereign Initiator, publicly revealed himself through what he made. The creation itself displays his nature and glory (Ps. 10:1; Rom. 1:20–23), but he revealed himself in a unique way by creating Adam and Eve in his own image (Gen. 1:26–27). Thus God's self-revelation provides the fundamental basis for worship.

God created Adam and Eve not simply to be a revelation of himself; he created them to nurture a relationship with them, to dwell with them in perfect communion. To do this, God created the Garden of Eden (Gen. 2:8) as a sanctuary in which he could walk with Adam and Eve (Gen. 3:8).

Humankind's purpose in this sanctuary was to "work it and keep it" (Gen. 2:15). Hebrew scholars note that the underlying terms in this statement mean far more than a gardener's task, a fact which the absence of thorns and weeds at this juncture in human history makes clear. For example, Allen Ross notes that the first verb, *avid*, is "used frequently for spiritual service, specifically serving the LORD (Deut. 4:19) and for the duties of the Levites (see Num. 3:7–8; 4:23–24, 26)." Likewise with the second verb, *shamar*, "its religious use is that of observing spiritual duties or keeping the commandments (Lev. 18:5)." With this in mind, Ross observes:

> In places where these two verbs are found together, they often refer to the duties of the Levites (cf. Num. 3:7–8; 8:26; 18:5–6), keeping the laws of God (especially in the sanctuary service) and offering spiritual service in the form of the sacrifices and all the related duties—serving the LORD, safeguarding his

commands, and guarding the sanctuary from the intrusion of anything profane or evil.[1]

Thus basic ideas about the nature and function of what would later become formal, corporate worship were established in the Creation event: God reveals himself through his creation and places Adam and Eve in the sanctuary of the garden where he dwells with them and walks with them in communion as they serve him and keep his commandments. This relationship between God and man does not exist for its own sake, but rather it brings glory to the Creator (Isa. 43:6–7). As the image-bearers walk with him and obey his commands, they evidence a complete satisfaction and trust in him, thus giving him ultimate praise.

Adam and Eve's fall into sin—their disobedience of God's commandments—was essentially failure to express dependence and satisfaction in their Creator and bring him glory, and thus it was a failure to worship him acceptably. This broke the communion they had with God and propelled them from the sanctuary of his presence. After they sinned, and they heard God walking in the garden, "the man and his wife hid themselves from the presence of the LORD God" (Gen. 3:8)—they recognized their unworthiness to walk with him. Their sin created a separation between them and their Creator, and they were forced to leave the sanctuary (Gen. 3:23–24), never again able to draw as near to the presence of God.

Yet before God drove them from the garden, he initiated a solution to the broken communion. First, he enacted a covenant with them wherein he promised redemption (Gen. 3:15). Then, he pictured that redemption through atonement by slaying an animal and covering Adam and Eve's guilt with its skin (Gen. 3:21). This atonement restored the broken relationship and once again enabled communion with God, although now limited. Timothy M. Pierce provides a helpful explanation of how "atonement" is directly connected to restoring communion with God:

> The English word "atonement" originated in the sixteenth century. It was not borrowed from another language, but was created in order to express an idea for which no word existed. The

---

1. Allen Ross, *Recalling the Hope of Glory: Biblical Worship from the Garden to the New Creation* (Grand Rapids: Kregel, 2006), 105–6.

combination of the words "at-one-ment" expressed the idea of reconciliation whereby not just agreement was achieved, but essential unity was acquired.[2]

Thus in the Creation/Fall event each of the essential elements of worship appear in seed form: (1) God reveals himself and initiates a relationship with his people; (2) God forms the boundaries of the relationship with his commandments; (3) the nature of worship consists in this relationship of communion between man and his Creator; (4) this worship takes place in the sanctuary of God's presence; (5) failure to obey the commandments of God prohibits communion with him; (6) God provides atonement whereby man is once again enabled to walk in communion with him.

These elements persist throughout Scripture even as their external manifestations become at times more complex and specific. The Exodus of Israel and the establishment of the Mosaic Law in a sense codify these elements that had been established at Creation. Once again, God was the initiator of the contact through his self-revelation in the burning bush (Ex. 3:1–2). The purpose of this meeting was to reestablish a relationship between God and his people (Ex. 3:7–8), but sin prevented Moses from fully drawing near to God's presence—God commanded him, "Do not come near; take your sandals off your feet, for the place on which you are standing is holy ground" (Ex. 3:5).

God accomplished his people's deliverance from bondage through atonement in the Passover event (Ex. 12:1–32). He led them out of Egypt with his own presence in the form of pillars of cloud and fire (Ex. 13:21–22) to the foot of Mt. Sinai, where he revealed himself to them (Ex. 19:9), "all the congregation *drew near* and stood before the Lord" (Lev. 9:5), and God spoke to them "face to face" (Deut. 5:4). Because of the sinfulness of the people, however, God placed clear limits on how closely the people could draw near to him (Ex. 19:12–13, 21–25), Moses alone serving as a mediator between the people and God (Ex. 24:2).

God's instructions concerning the construction of the tabernacle also reveal a visualization of the worship elements that had been instituted at

2. Timothy M. Pierce, *Enthroned on Our Praise: An Old Testament Theology of Worship* (Nashville: B&H Publishing Group, 2008), 75n105.

Creation. This structure served as a sanctuary for God's presence ("And let them make me a sanctuary, that I may dwell in their midst," Ex. 25:8)—drawing near to the tabernacle was to draw near to the very presence of God himself, and each piece of furniture within the tabernacle symbolized both the presence of God and the relationship of communion that he desired with his people. The table of acacia wood (Ex. 25:23–30) signified such communion with God since in the ancient Near East dining with someone portrayed complete fellowship with that person.[3] Likewise, the golden lampstand (Ex. 25:31–39) represented the presence of God in two possible ways: first, it reminded the people of the light that God created and thus symbolized his presence.[4] Second, Carol Meyers suggests that the lampstand also symbolized the tree of life, harkening back to the garden sanctuary and further reminding the people of communion in God's sanctuary.[5] The altar of incense (Ex. 30:1–5) represented the intercessory prayers of God's people (Ps. 141:2; Rev. 8:3–5) and thus also emphasized dialogue in relationship with him. Finally, the Ark of the Covenant (Ex. 25:10–22) was the center of God's presence ("There will I meet with you," Ex. 25:22).

Yet once again, because of the guilt of the people, barriers prevented them from drawing fully near to communion with God in his presence. The curtain surrounding the outer court prevented unlawful approach to God's presence (Ex. 27:9–19). Only appointed priests entered the tabernacle itself (Ex. 30:7–10; Lev. 24–25). Finally, God commanded that a veil be hung separating the Holy Place from the Most Holy, the chamber holding the ark and the very presence of God (Ex. 26:33). Only the High Priest was permitted to enter that place, and only once a year on the Day of Atonement (Lev. 16:1–19; cf. Heb. 9:7). Thus God initiated a system of sacrifices in order to provide atonement and at least partial and temporary access to his presence (Lev. 1–9).

However, what the tabernacle also reveals is that these essential worship elements were not simply instituted at Creation, but are in fact representations of the essence of the worship in Heaven itself. God gives Moses

---

3. Allen P. Ross, *Holiness to the Lord: A Guide to the Exposition of the Book of Leviticus* (Grand Rapids: Baker, 2006), 30.
4. John I. Durham, *Exodus* (Waco, TX: Word Books, 1987), 362–63.
5. Carol L. Meyers, *The Tabernacle Menorah: A Synthetic Study of a Symbol from the Biblical Cult* (Piscataway, NJ: Gorgias Press LLC, 2003), 96, 118–19, 133.

the pattern (Ex. 25:8–9; 25:40; 27:8; Num. 8:4; cf. Acts 7:44), and this is a pattern of "heavenly things" (Heb. 8:2, 5; cf. Heb. 9:11, 23–24). In other words, the idea of worship visualized at Creation and in the tabernacle (and later, the temple) is modeled after the eternal essence of heavenly worship. This means that the worship construct observed at Creation and illustrated through the Mosaic system reveals the essence of worship: (1) God reveals himself and initiates a relationship with his people; (2) God forms the boundaries of the relationship with his commandments; (3) the nature of worship consists in this relationship of communion between man and his Creator; (4) this worship takes place in the sanctuary of God's presence; (5) failure to obey the commandments of God prohibits communion with him; (6) God provides atonement whereby man is once again enabled to walk in communion with him.

Drawing Near through Christ

Taking into account this essential picture of worship as expressed in both Creation and the Mosaic system allows for a more complete recognition of the significance of Christ's coming for the overall understanding of the nature of Christian worship. Jesus himself revealed his deep identification with the temple by the fact that he cleansed it both at the beginning (John 2:13–15) and end (Mark 11:15–19; 11:27–33; Matt. 21:12–17; 21:23–27; Luke 19:45–48; 20:1–8) of his earthly ministry.

Yet he is not so much tied to the external rituals of the temple worship (although he participates regularly in them while on earth); he is concerned with what happens at the temple because of the deeper importance of what it signifies. This is made clear by his discussion with the Samaritan woman (John 4:7–26). He indicates that although location was necessary as part of the Mosaic system ("We worship what we know, for salvation is from the Jews," John 4:22), his coming removes the necessity of that system since it is only a visualization of the deeper spiritual realities of worship ("But the hour is coming, and is now here, when the true worshipers will worship the Father in spirit and truth, for the Father is seeking such people to worship him," John 4:23). This also allows him to emphasize the nature of communion with God and his people as one of dialogue—God speaks ("truth"), and his people respond with their spirits.

Consequently, Christ's coming clearly shifts the emphasis from external ritual and location that had come to characterize the Mosaic system to an emphasis upon the essential nature of worship and Christ's role in it. This emphasis is perhaps most thoroughly explained in the book of Hebrews. Therefore, a careful study of the message of the book of Hebrews reveals a well-developed theology of Christian worship and, in particular, lays an important foundation for an understanding of the relationship between worship and evangelism.

Drawing Near in Hebrews

Peter Rhea Jones argues that two minor climaxes in the literary structure of Hebrews that lead to a final climax in 12:18–29 reveal that the primary theme of the entire book is a call to "come near and worship."[6] The first climax occurs in 4:16: "Let us then with confidence *draw near* [*proserchōmetha*] to the throne of grace," and the second in 10:22: "Let us *draw near* [*proserchōmetha*] with a true heart in full assurance of faith." The same concept in slightly different form appears in the final climax in 12:22: "But you *have come* [*proselēlythate*] to Mount Zion." Jones thus notes that "this imagistic portrayal of distinctive Christian worship enjoys a dramatic location in the epistle,"[7] and the idea of "drawing near" is at the heart of the author's concept of worship. William Lane suggests that the verb form of this term used in verse 12:18, *proserchomai*, is more than simply a casual expression of "coming," but rather "is used exclusively of an approach to God. The writer compares Israel's approach to God in cultic ceremony to the Christian's experience in worship."[8] The term's close connection with the idea of worship is illustrated by its use in the Greek translation of the Old Testament to describe the approach of priests to God for the performing of their Levitical duties.[9]

---

6. Peter Rhea Jones, "A Superior Life: Hebrews 12:3–13:25," *Review and Expositor* 82, no. 3 (1985): 396.
7. Ibid., 397.
8. William Lane, *Hebrews* (Dallas: Word Books, 1991), 460.
9. Brenda B. Colijn, "'Let Us Approach': Soteriology in the Epistle to the Hebrews," *Journal of the Evangelical Theological Society* 39, no. 4 (December 1996): 570–86; W. Mundle, "ἔρχομαι," in *New International Dictionary of New Testament Theology*, ed. Colin Brown, ed., vol. 1 (Grand Rapids: Zondervan, 1986); J. Schneider, "ἔρχομαι," in *Theological Dictionary of the New Testament: Index*, ed. Kittel Gerhard and Friedrich Gerhard, vol. 2 (Grand Rapids: Wm. B. Eerdmans, 1976).\\uc0\\u8221{} \\i Journal of the Evangelical Theological Society\\ i0{} 39, no. 4 (December 1996

This concept of drawing near to the presence of God as the essence of worship is what was first introduced at Creation and later in the establishment of the tabernacle, and this experience characterized worship from the Fall until Christ's sacrifice: God calls his people to draw near to communion with him in his sanctuary, they cannot because of their sin, and he provides limited access through sacrificial atonement. Only those who trust in his promises and present a sacrifice can truly worship.

Yet the book of Hebrews reveals the radical change that occurred in this understanding of worship because of Christ. The rhetorical climax of the book, 12:18–29, provides a good example of the discontinuity between approaching God in each covenant. The contrast is between two mountains as representative of the two ways of approaching God—the way people had to draw near to him under the Law and the way Christians come to worship because of Christ. Verses 18–24 present the contrast:

> For you have not come [*proselēlythate*] to what may be touched, a blazing fire and darkness and gloom and a tempest and the sound of a trumpet and a voice whose words made the hearers beg that no further messages be spoken to them. For they could not endure the order that was given, "If even a beast touches the mountain, it shall be stoned." Indeed, so terrifying was the sight that Moses said, "I tremble with fear." But you have come [*proselēlythate*] to Mount Zion and to the city of the living God, the heavenly Jerusalem, and to innumerable angels in festal gathering, and to the assembly of the firstborn who are enrolled in heaven, and to God, the judge of all, and to the spirits of the righteous made perfect, and to Jesus, the mediator of a new covenant, and to the sprinkled blood that speaks a better word than the blood of Abel.

The author's descriptions of these two contrasting mountains are instructive and important to his argument, highlighted by the emphatic position of the negative term *ou* ("not") in verse 18 and the strongly negative term *alla* ("on the contrary") in verse 22. Clearly something significant has changed between worship under Law and worship through Christ.

No Greek word for "mountain" actually appears in verse 18, yet the idea is clearly implied in the context as a contrast to "Mount Zion" in verse 22.

The author has in mind here Mount Sinai and the giving of the Law. He tells his readers that as Christians they "have not come" to this Old Testament mountain, which represents religion under the Law; rather they have come to "Mount Zion." The latter mountain often refers in Scripture to the physical location of Jerusalem, but the context as well as the synonym "heavenly Jerusalem" clearly demonstrates that the author is using the term in a figurative sense to represent the "city of the living God."

This is the mountain to which these believers "have come," but they have not come to this mountain physically—at least not yet. They still live on the physical earth, but in Christ they have come to this mountain in a spiritual sense; they are "raised ... up with him and seated ... with him in the heavenly places" (Eph. 2:6). God is present on this mountain, just as he had been on Sinai, but the experience is quite different. On this mountain gather beings not currently present on earth but rather those who reside in heaven with God himself. Most importantly, Jesus himself resides on this mountain, providing the means by which Christians are present there, for in Christ they have been positionally seated in this realm.

In Hebrews 12:18, Mount Sinai stands as a representative for worship under the Law, and thus the location of this worship is first the tabernacle and later the temple. In contrast, worship for a Christian takes place on "Mount Zion, even the city of the living God, the heavenly Jerusalem" (12:22). These synonymous terms refer to the heavenly city, the place where God himself dwells, which is made clear by the groups of participants there: joyful angels, "the assembly of the firstborn," God, and "the spirits of the righteous made perfect" (vv 22–23). The term *ekklēsia*, translated "assembly" in verse 22 likely refers to the common sense of New Testament "church" and thus designates post-Pentecost believers, while the latter phrase describes Old Testament saints now "made perfect" by the atonement of Christ's blood.[10] So the company of worshipers in this heavenly scene includes angels, New Testament Christians, and Old Testament believers. Here in this heavenly city God actually dwells; the worshipers come to him rather than him coming down to them as in the Sinai experience and his presence in the tabernacle and temple.

---

10. Homer Kent, *The Epistle to the Hebrews: A Commentary* (Grand Rapids: Baker Book House, 1972), 273.

The author of Hebrews contrasts these worship locations in a number of ways throughout the book. He distinguishes between "the true tent that the Lord set up" and the one set up by man (8:1–2). This heavenly tent is "greater and more perfect" since it is "not made with hands, that is, not of this creation" (9:11). He calls the earthly places of worship and all that they entail "copies of the heavenly things" (9:23) and "copies of the true things" (9:24). The Law in general is "a shadow of the good things to come instead of the true form of these realities" (10:1).

The discontinuity between these locations of worship is not, however, a decisive one. Rather, the book of Hebrews develops the understanding that such physical locations of worship in the Old Testament economy were prototypes of the actual worship in heaven, where Christians are now seated through Christ. The tent set up by man and the human sacrifices "serve a copy and shadow of the heavenly things" (8:5); Moses had been instructed to construct the earthly tent according to a "pattern" of the heavenly temple. Thus a thorough knowledge and understanding of Old Testament worship is critically relevant for the New Testament Church, for it illustrates some of the spiritual realities of heavenly worship and especially pictures the essence of worship as drawing near to the presence of God.

The author of Hebrews uses this idea of "drawing near" throughout the book to describe approaching God in worship. Hebrews 4:16 highlights that the coming of Christians to God in worship is based upon grace, leading to a boldness that the Hebrews at Sinai could not express: "Let us then with confidence *draw near (proserchōmetha)* to the throne of grace." Hebrews 7:25 emphasizes the fact that Christ's high priestly ministry of intercession makes such an approach possible: "Consequently, he is able to save to the uttermost those who *draw near (proserchomenous)* to God through him, since he always lives to make intercession for them." In 10:1, the author reveals the insufficiency of animal sacrifices to purify those who come to God in worship: "For since the law has but a shadow of the good things to come instead of the true form of these realities, it can never, by the same sacrifices that are continually offered every year, make perfect those who *draw near (proserchomenous)*." In contrast, 10:22 proclaims that since believers in Christ have "a great high priest," they may "*draw near (proserchōmetha)* with a true heart in full assurance of faith, with [their] hearts sprinkled clean from an evil conscience and [their] bodies washed with pure water." Hebrews 11:6 further emphasizes the need for faith in coming to God in worship (more below): "And without faith it is impossible to please him, for whoever would *draw near* (*proserchomenon*) to God must believe that he exists and that he rewards those who seek him."

Drawing near to the presence of God is the fundamental experience of worship for God's people under both covenants, and it is the essence of worship (in both a personal or corporate sense). Descriptions of this approach with relation to the Old Covenant are always negative, however (10:1; 12:18), since those attempting to worship have not been purified; God is essentially unapproachable. In contrast, approach to God in the New Testament is indeed possible because it is mediated by Jesus Christ and is based upon his sacrifice; therefore, Christians can come with boldness and joy. This contrast of response in approaching God is best summarized by the descriptions in 12:18–24. The Hebrews at Sinai "could not endure" the experience, yet Christians worshiping spiritually in the heavenly temple enter a "festal gathering."

Worship Initiated by God's Self-Revelation

Throughout the book, the author of Hebrews highlights the fact that this worship is rooted in God's initiative and his own revelation, but he also reveals the essential discontinuity between revelation under the Old Testament and revelation for the Church. Old Testament saints relied heavily upon supernatural, transient means through which to receive revelation from God. The first verse of the book notes what would have been for the Jews the primary source of revelation—prophets. Yet as unique and authoritative as these messengers of God's word were to the Jews, the supreme messenger is now the Word himself (John 1:1). This source of divine revelation "is the radiance of the glory of God and the exact imprint of his nature, and he upholds the universe by the word of his power" (1:3). In other words, he is not simply a messenger of God's revelation— he *is* God and he *is* the revelation. In fact, in verse 2, there is no article before "Son." As Morris notes:

> In essence the writer is saying God spoke "in one who has the quality of being Son." It is the Son's essential nature that is stressed. This stands in contrast to "the prophets" in the preceding verse. The consummation of the revelatory process,

the definitive revelation, took place when he who was not one of "the goodly fellowship of the prophets" but the very Son of God came.[11]

The author focuses on another source of revelation in chapters one and two—angels. The Jews considered these mysterious beings as special, visible representations of God's word. In contrast to what his readers would have considered the supreme sources of revelation and thus images of the authority of God, the author exalts Jesus Christ as superior, both as the source of revelation and as the very person of God himself.

This verbal revelation is essentially the basis for drawing near to God. The Word from God delivered through prophets or heavenly messengers was the only means through which Old Testament believers could worship the Lord. Without these supernatural insertions into the earthly realm, people had insufficient knowledge for communion with the Creator. Even then, this knowledge was lacking, for it came sporadically and, at times, impersonally. Yet with the coming of Christ, the revelation that provided a *foundation* for communion was also both the *object* and the *basis* of that communion.

The Basis for Drawing Near in Worship

Hebrews also presents the idea of atonement sacrifice as that which makes drawing near to God in worship possible. God required Old Testament saints to offer sacrifices with him as means of temporary forgiveness. These sacrifices themselves were imperfect, and they did nothing to change the heart of the one offering the sacrifice. They did not provide full atonement (10:4, 11), but rather a temporary, legal satisfaction of immediate wrath. They could not cleanse sin, but they could "sanctify for the cleansing of the flesh" (9:13). Although these Old Testament sacrifices were limited, they served as "copies" (9:23) of the perfect, complete sacrifice that was to come in the person of Jesus Christ. Thus the means to draw near in worship in the Old Testament was limited and only temporary.

In contrast, the climax of Hebrews in 12:24 directs the reader's attention to "the sprinkled blood" of Jesus as the basis for New Testament

---

11. Leon Morris, "Hebrews," in *The Expositor's Bible Commentary, Hebrews–Revelation*, ed. Frank E. Gaebelein (Grand Rapids: Zondervan, 1981), 13.

worship. This idea of sprinkling is intricately tied to the ratification of the covenant and harkens back to the sprinkling that confirmed the old covenant (9:19–21). Yet the blood is a synecdoche for the whole of Christ's sacrificial death, which is made clear by its comparison to another violent murder of an innocent victim—that of Abel. According the Hebrews, Abel "is still speaking, although he died" (11:4), and yet the blood of Christ "continues to speak more effectively" (12:24) as a final sacrifice of atonement that makes worship possible. This sacrifice of Christ is an act of grace rather than vengeance as Abel's had been.

Christ is not only the sacrifice, however; he is also the priest who offers the sacrifice. The author highlights this truth as one of the first descriptions of the Son of God in 1:3, noting that after Christ made "purification for sins, he sat down at the right hand of the Majesty on high." The term "purification" (*katharismon*) is most often used in the New Testament to refer to ritual cleansing, yet in this case it has direct reference to the removal of sin by the sacrifice of Christ.[12] This act of offering one sacrifice and then sitting is in stark contrast to the work of Old Testament priests who had to offer continual sacrifices (10:11–12). The author reiterates this fact in 7:27: "He has no need, like those high priests, to offer sacrifices daily, first for his own sins and then for those of the people, since he did this once for all when he offered up himself." Their sacrifice did not remove sin, but Christ's did. The author of Hebrews speaks of this act of removing sin completely several times throughout the book. Jesus made "propitiation for the sins of the people" (2:17); his sacrifice ensured that God would remember the sins of his people no more (8:12; 10:17); he was "offered once to bear the sins of many" (9:28); he "offered for all time a single sacrifice for sin" (10:12); he made an "offering for sin" (10:18); he "appeared once for all at the end of the ages to put away sin by the sacrifice of himself" (9:26); his death brought redemption from transgression (9:15). Throughout the book, the author stresses that the Old Covenant could not remove sin, but now Christ has accomplished full atonement (10:2, 4, 6, 11).

The author portrays Jesus Christ as the bridge between physical and spiritual realities. Christ is able to serve as the high priest of his people because he was both "made like his brothers in every respect" (2:17), and, having "passed through the heavens" (4:14), he "is seated at the right

---

12. Ibid., 15.

hand of the throne of the Majesty in heaven, a minister in the holy places, in the true tent that the Lord set up, not man" (8:1–2). There he entered, "not by means of the blood of goats and calves but by means of his own blood, thus securing an eternal redemption" (9:12). Physical beings would not be able to worship an eternal God without a mediator who is both physical and eternal; in this sense, as Torrance explains,

> the real agent in all true worship is Jesus Christ. He is our great high priest and ascended Lord, the one true worshiper who unites us to himself by the Spirit in an act of memory and in a life of communion, as he lifts us up by word and sacrament into the very triune life of God.[13]

The Means of Drawing Near in Worship

Faith stands in Hebrews as the supreme continuity between Old Testament and New Testament worship since it functions as an essential link between the physical and spiritual. The author of Hebrews defines faith as "the assurance of things *hoped for*, the conviction of things *not seen*" (11:1). Two modifiers in the author's definition of faith reveal its connection between physical and spiritual. First, Morris argues that *hypostasis* ("assurance") has the idea that faith is the basis by which we know spiritual reality. He explains:

> His meaning is that there are realities for which we have no material evidence though they are not the less real for that. Faith enables us to know that they exist and, while we have no certainty apart from faith, faith does give us genuine certainty. ... Faith is the basis, the substructure (*hypostasis* means lit. "that which stands under") of all that the Christian life means, all that the Christian hopes for.[14]

The second word that draws a connection between the physical and the spiritual is *elegchos* ("conviction"), which has the idea of testing something—in this case, "things not seen." The author's point is that faith is what allows

---

13. James Torrance, *Worship, Community, and the Triune God of Grace* (Downers Grove, IL: Inter-Varsity Press, 1996), 17.
14. Morris, "Hebrews," 113.

physical beings to both know and test spiritual reality. He removes all doubt of his emphasis in 11:3: "By faith we understand that the universe was created by the word of God, so that what *is seen* was not made out of things that are *visible.*" Faith is the basis for knowing and testing spiritual truth. Without this faith, "it is impossible to please [God], for whoever would draw near to God must believe that he exists and that he rewards those who seek him" (11:6). No physical person can see God or his rewards, but faith allows true believers to know and have confidence in them even though they cannot experience them with their physical senses; thus faith allows a believer to "draw near" to God in worship spiritually.

The great "faith chapter" of Hebrews (chapter 11) highlights, then, Old Testament saints who exhibited true faith, and several cases specifically express how these saints believed in spiritual realities that they could not perceive with their physical senses. For example, Noah obeyed God's instructions even though what he was warned of was yet "*unseen*" (11:7). Abraham, too, obeyed God, even though he did not "know where he was going" (11:8); instead, "he was looking forward to the city that has foundations, *whose designer and builder is God*" (11:10), that spiritual kingdom described in 12:18–29. Joseph rested in confidence in a future exodus for the Hebrew people, even though he did not experience it himself (11:22). Moses "left Egypt, not being afraid of the anger of the king, for he endured *as seeing him who is invisible*" (11:27). Even Jesus himself is set up as an example of one who "endured the cross" because he was looking forward to the spiritual "*joy that was set before him*" (12:2). In each of these demonstrations of faith, God's true worshipers did not rely on what they could see or touch—in fact, they never experienced the fulfillment of what they had been promised in this life. Instead "these all died in faith, not having received the things promised, but having seen them and greeted them *from afar*" (11:13); they desired "a *better country*"—not a physical one but "a *heavenly* one" (11:16) They did not rely on their physical senses but rather on the only sense that can perceive the spiritual—faith.

The Consequences of Refusing to Draw Near through Christ

The five warning passages in Hebrews (2:1–4; 3:1–4:13; 5:11–6:20; 10:26–29; 12:14–29) stand as an important part of the author's argument and reveal one of the prominent continuities between the Old and New Testaments. The author of Hebrews does not relate judgment as present only in the old economy; the consequences of rejecting true worship are the same in both Testaments.

Hebrews 12:18–29 itself functions not only as the summary and conclusion of the book's main body but also as the author's final statement of warning—"See that you do not refuse him who is speaking" (v. 25)—and this warning is rooted in a grave continuity between Old Testament and New Testament worship. The author proclaims that the same judge who descended to earth in order to judge those who rejected him will also judge from his place in the heavenly city. Lane notes that "the form of the argument is precisely that of 2:2–3a,"[15] which is the first warning of the book: "For since the message declared by angels proved to be reliable, and every transgression or disobedience received a just retribution, how shall we escape if we neglect such a great salvation?" This reveals an *inclusio* structure of the book and highlights these warnings as critical to the author's purpose. In both of these warnings, the author draws on the continuities between the Old Testament and New Testament to demonstrate the reality of certain judgment for those who refuse to worship as God has intended. The other three warning passages are equally as forceful, magnifying the author's concern that his readers not reject Christian worship in favor of that of Judaism. The point is clear: those who refuse to worship Christ will find judgment, but those who do worship him will receive forgiveness and life everlasting.

Defining Christian Worship

Each of the essential elements of worship seen in Creation and the tabernacle are present in Hebrews' explanation of Christian worship: (1) God reveals himself and initiates a relationship with his people; (2) God forms the boundaries of the relationship with his commandments; (3) the nature of worship consists in this relationship of communion between man and his Creator; (4) this worship takes place in the sanctuary of God's presence; (5) failure to obey the commandments of God prohibits communion with him; (6) God provides atonement whereby man is once again enabled to walk in communion with him. Yet added revelation concerning Jesus Christ takes the potential of truly drawing near to God in communion beyond mere hope (as after the Fall) or a temporary and lim-

---

15. Lane, *Hebrews*, 477.

ited possibility (as in the Mosaic system) to full reality. Thus the theology of Christian worship from the book of Hebrews is that Christian worship is drawing near to God through Jesus Christ by faith.

What should be apparent from this study is that the essence of worship is itself the language of the gospel—a drawing near to God in relationship with him, made impossible because of sin that demands eternal judgment, yet restored through the substitutionary atonement of the God-man for those who place their faith in him. Already the biblical relationship between worship and mission appears clearer since worship and the gospel are essentially connected. The gospel of Jesus Christ makes worship possible.

The Significance of Corporate Worship

Thus far the discussion of worship, defined in terms of the believer's relationship to God through Christ, applies to the entirety of a Christian's life and may give the impression that there is nothing distinct or sacred about corporate worship. Indeed, this is exactly what many missional authors insist.[16] As cultural transformationalists they view all of life as worship, and thus the Sunday morning gathering of the church is in essence no different from what goes on the other six days of the week—it all fits under the scope of the *missio Dei*.

Several problems with this perspective exist, however, deserving careful consideration. First, the nature of the church must be defined biblically. While it is true that "church" in the New Testament sometimes refers to the universal number of believers in Christ,[17] it most often refers specifically to a local gathering of such believers. For example, Paul addressed letters "to the church of God that is in Corinth (1 Cor. 1:2; 2 Cor. 1:1), "to the churches of Galatia" (Gal. 1:2), and "to the church of the Thessalonians" (1 Thess. 1:1). This raises at least two important points: first, a church is an identifiable group of *believers* in Christ; unbelievers are not part of churches. Second, a church is a *gathering* of believers in Christ; a church does not exist except when it is gathered. In other words, most of the discussion of "church" in the New Testament refers to "church

---

16. See Driscoll, *Religion Saves*, 253.
17. See, for example, Matthew 16:18; Ephesians 1:22–23; 3:10; 3:21; 4:4; 5:23–27; 1 Corinthians 10:32; 11:22; 12:28; Colossians 1:18, 24; Hebrews 12:23.

as institution" rather than "church as organism" (to use Kuyper's terms). Furthermore, one cannot really speak of the "church as organism" except in the sense of the "universal church"; Christians are not "the church" as described in most New Testament cases when they act outside the regular workings of the local church. Thus, discussions of the "mission" of the church or whether worship in a gathering of the church is distinct from worship as Christian living must take this into account.

Understanding the church to be a distinct, gathered group of believers in Christ, recognition of the various terms used in the New Testament to describe this gathered church is quite instructive. For example, Paul tells Timothy that he is writing so that "you may know how one ought to be-have in the household of God, which is the church of the living God" (1 Tim. 3:15).[18] The term "household of God" (*oikō theou*) is used throughout Scripture to refer to a special place of God's presence. For example, Jacob calls the place where he met with God "Bethel, "or "house of God" (Gen. 28:10–22). Likewise the tabernacle is often called the "house of God" (Judg. 18:30, 1 Chron. 9:25–27), as is the temple (2 Chron. 3:3, Ps .52:8, Ezra 4:24, Neh. 13:11, Matt. 12:4, Mark 2:26, and, Luke 6:4). The church is also called specifically the "temple" (*naós*; 1 Cor. 3:16–17, 2 Cor. 6:16, Eph. 2:19–22). Thus when believers gather as the church, they exist in some spe-cial way as the dwelling place of God—the sanctuary of worship—so that, as Jesus promised, "where two or three are gathered in my name, there am I among them" (Matt. 18:20). Although individual believers are also called "a temple of the Holy Spirit" (1 Cor. 6:19–20), the context and plural pro-nouns in each of the aforementioned cases clearly refer to when individual believers gather as the church. So there is a special sense of being the sanctu-ary of God that exists only when the church is gathered, rather than at other times. This alone should give indication of something sacred and distinct for the gathered church, with strong emphasis upon worship signified by the use of Old Testament worship terminology.

Finally, as was already mentioned earlier, Paul indicates to Tim-othy that there is a certain way "to behave in the household of God" (1 Tim. 3:15). Something about the assembled church requires particular behavior that is set apart from behavior in the rest of life. So while an individual Christian is the temple of God's spirit and ought to behave in

---

18. See also Hebrews 10:19–24.

ways that are pleasing to him, the church gathered is, in a special and distinct way, the sanctuary of God's presence, wherein God's people behave in worship differently than in any other circumstances. For this reason, behavior in the church must be regulated by God's clear instructions in a way more explicit than for behavior outside the church.

One of the ways this takes place is that corporate worship is the public acting out of the spiritual realities of worship; it is a weekly dramatic re-creation of drawing near to God through Christ by faith. Bryan Chapell presents a convincing historical argument along these lines in *Christ-Centered Worship*. By comparing and contrasting the most influential Christian liturgies in the history of Christianity, Chapell demonstrates that although these various liturgies certainly differ as they reflect the specifics of the theological systems in which they operate, "where the truths of the gospel are maintained there remain commonalities of worship structure that transcend culture."[19] He shows that no matter the differences, each liturgy contains common elements: adoration, confession, assurance, thanksgiving, petition, instruction, charge, and blessing. Not only are the elements common, but their progression also remains consistent among the liturgies. Chapell argues that this is the case because each liturgy "reflects the pattern of the progress of the gospel in the heart."[20] A person recognizes the greatness of God (adoration), which leads him to see his need for confession of sin. He then receives assurance of pardon in the gospel through the merits of Christ, and he responds with thanksgiving and petition. God then gives his Word in response to the petition (instruction), leading to a charge to obey its teaching and promise of blessing. This common liturgical structure, telling the story of the gospel, "re-presents" the gospel—drawing near to God through Christ by faith— each time God's people worship.

The climax of this gospel-shaped worship is communion around the Lord's Table. Throughout Scripture (and, indeed, history), the ultimate expression of free and open access is being invited to sit at the table. This is illustrated throughout the Old Testament, it is pictured with the Table of Showbread in the Temple, and it is one of the beautiful images depicted by the Lord's Supper. A Christian worship service pictures that believers are

---

19. Bryan Chapell, *Christ-Centered Worship: Letting the Gospel Shape Our Practice* (Grand Rapids: Baker Academic, 2009), 18.
20. Ibid., 99.

accepted through Christ, and now sitting around his table both commemorates the sacrifice that made that possible *and* expresses our unity with him and with other Christians as the body of Christ. It does not accomplish peace with God, as Rome teaches; rather, it is a beautiful expression of peace already achieved through the sacrifice of Christ. This is why the Table is the ultimate climax of any gospel-shaped worship service. In the Table, Christians are enabled to sit in full communion with their Sovereign Lord because of Christ. The Lord's Table is the most beautiful earthly enactment of the complete fellowship made possible by union with Christ.

Worship on Earth as It Is in Heaven

Christians need not weep, because the true locus of worship is not a physical Temple in a particular earthly location from which we are separated due to captivity in a foreign land. No, these were but shadows of true spiritual worship that takes place in the Temple of heaven itself. And because of our relationship with Christ, who even now sits in that Temple, we do not need to long to be present there so that we can sing what rightly belongs there. Rather, whenever we draw near to God through Christ by faith, we are spiritually entering the heavenly Jerusalem and joining with the festal worship of angels and saints who have gone before us.

We are still in a strange land, but we can sing the songs of Zion *in* Zion spiritually as we worship with Christ even now.

chapter 9

ZION'S SONG

Great is the LORD and greatly to be praised
in the city of our God!
His holy mountain, beautiful in elevation,
is the joy of all the earth,
Mount Zion, in the far north,
the city of the great King.
Psalm 48:1–2

Worship and the Mission of God

The missional church movement has attempted to explain the connection between worship and redemption, but what this discussion has shown is that the missional understanding has several important problems. First, as an understanding of worship in Hebrews makes clear, redemption is subordinate to the end of worship since the gospel exists to create worshipers. The ultimate end of worship existed prior to the fall of Adam and Eve into sin; that end would have existed regardless of their rebellion. The end of redemption, on the other hand, exists only after the fall. Scripture is clear that God does delight in redemption of his people, but it also serves a further ultimate end, that of creating worshipers. God redeems his people for the purpose of gaining them access to full communion with himself, thus causing them to delight in him and praise him. Even though redemption is a primary purpose in the work of God, it is subordinate to the ultimate end of worship. Therefore, God's mission is to create worshipers, and he accomplishes this mission through the gospel.

Second, even if God's mission of redemption is an important purpose in his work, God's mission and the mission of the church are not the same. Missional advocates, often citing John 20:21, insist these in an equality between the two. But the church's mission is never explained in Scripture in terms of *redemption*—especially in terms of redeeming culture; rather, the church's mission is to make disciples.

In fact, David M. Doran suggests that "we should... [question] the somewhat arbitrary choice to make John 17:18 and 20:21 the definitive texts regarding mission."[1] He continues:

> In light of the unmistakable emphasis in all of the other commission texts on proclamation, it seems very strained to redefine mission on the basis of these two somewhat obscure texts. By obscure, I mean that they do not specify the nature of our commission, that is, they do not at all tell us *what* we are to do. In terms of biblical interpretation, the proper way to approach the issue of mission would be to correlate all of the commission texts by moving from the clearest texts to the more obscure.[2]

Instead, Doran suggests that the Great Commission of Matthew 28:18–20 reveals the Lord's "desire for the church during the [church age]."[3]

Kevin DeYoung and Greg Gilbert agree, including also Mark 13:10, Mark 14:9, Luke 24:44–49, and Acts 1:8 as texts that are part of the Great Commission.[4] They argue that the church should limit its understanding of its mission to these key texts since not everything God is doing in the world is necessarily also the task of the church. Rather, they insist that the church's mission should rest "on Scripture's explicit commands."[5] These

---

1. David M. Doran, *For the Sake of His Name: Challenging a New Generation for World Missions* (Allen Park, MI: Student Global Impact, 2002), 103. Doran is specifically interacting with John Stott's interpretation and application of these texts as foundational to mission; see 97–102.
2. Ibid. Emphasis original.
3. Ibid., 71.
4. Kevin DeYoung and Greg Gilbert, *What Is the Mission of the Church? Making Sense of Social Justice, Shalom, and the Great Commission* (Wheaton: Crossway, 2011), 40.
5. Ibid., 41.

texts known as the Great Commission provide such explicit commands
for the church.

Treating the Matthew 28 occurrence, Doran argues that there is a single
command in the text, modified by other participial phrases, and that single
command is "make disciples of all nations."[6] Thus "go" is not strictly a command but rather the circumstances in which the primary command of making disciples finds its place.[7] Likewise "baptizing" and "teaching" describe
"characteristics of disciple making."[8] Doran argues that since making disciples is the primary command of the Great Commission, this task involves
not only the proclamation of the gospel but also teaching and nurturing
new converts; it "means to make someone into a learner or follower of Jesus
Christ. The commission given to us by Jesus involves the transformation
of rebels into followers. This means that, technically speaking, the Great
Commission involves more than what is normally called evangelism,"[9] by
which Doran means only leading someone to a decision for Christ. Shar-
ing the gospel is certainly the first step toward making disciples, but it is
not enough. Instead of understanding salvation to be a mere "intellectual
acceptance of certain biblical facts," Doran insists that

> saving faith sees the glory of God in the face of Jesus Christ
> (2 Cor. 4:6). Saving faith involves a heart response to the gos-
> pel where the affections are turned, by the Spirit, to him in
> love. … Saving faith also involves the will, that is, the believer
> embraces Jesus Christ as the only hope of eternal life and en-
> trusts himself to him.[10]

In other words, true conversion is not simply assent to certain facts; it
is a life-changing entrance into communion with God. It is "turn[ing]
to God from idols to serve a living and true God" (1 Thess. 1:9–10).[11]
Conversion is drawing near to God through Christ by faith, the essence
of Christian worship, and this results in change of behavior ("culture").

---

6. Doran, *For the Sake of His Name*, 73.
7. Doran does argue, however, that as an attendant participle, "go" does have some "imperatival
force" (ibid.).
8. Ibid., 74.
9. Ibid., 77.
10. Ibid., 82–83.
11. Cf. ibid., 85.

This leads to the third significant understanding regarding the relationship of worship to mission: even though the church's mission is to
make disciples through the proclamation of the gospel, this end is subordinate to worship. As John Piper has famously argued, "Missions exists
because worship doesn't."[12] In other words, the purpose of the gospel is to
enable people to draw near to communion with God through Christ by
faith, and making disciples involves bringing them into a deeper understanding of the nature of their relationship in worship to their Creator.
DeYoung and Gilbert's definition of the mission of the church includes
this essential relationship of mission to worship:

> The mission of the church is to go into the world and make
> disciples by declaring the gospel of Jesus Christ in the power of
> the Spirit and gathering these disciples into churches, that they
> might worship the Lord and obey his commands now and in
> eternity to the glory of God the Father.[13]

This definition is quite helpful since it includes an understanding that
evangelism ("declaring the gospel") is subordinate to making disciples,
which itself is subordinate to worship.

Finally, one more emphasis of the missional church movement must
be evaluated in light of God's ultimate ends. Not only do missional advocates seem to equate God's mission with the church's mission, but they
also define mission specifically as "sentness" rather than as redemption
or even evangelism. Everything about the church, according to missional
authors, should be subsumed under the higher end of being sent. For
example, Michael Frost argues:

> The whole idea of missional church thinking is a fundamental
> and prophetic call for the church to orient everything it is do-
> ing around the agenda of mission. In other words, of all the
> practices that the church ought to legitimately be involved in,
> missional church thinkers believe that mission ought to be the

---

12. John Piper, *Let the Nations Be Glad: The Supremacy of God in Missions*, 3rd ed. (Grand Rapids:
    Baker Academic, 2010), 35. Here Piper is using "missions" as the idea of evangelism rather
    than in the same way missional authors use "mission."
13. DeYoung and Gilbert, *What Is the Mission of the Church?*, 62.

organizing principle of all those things. We don't think that
worship is the primary organizing principle, though we think
worship is absolutely the mandate of the church. We don't think
that the creation of Christian fellowship or community is the
organizing principle, though we think that has absolute merit
as important. We don't even think that the expression evangelism is the primary organizing principle, although that is absolutely essential. When we talk about the missional church, we
are talking about which worship, community, leadership, evangelism, social justice, theological thinking is oriented around or
organized around the fundamental agenda of mission.[14]

In other words, for missional church advocates, mission is the highest
ultimate end, and everything else—including worship—is subordinate
to mission.

But this is precisely backwards. While redemption may be an ultimate
end for God, "sentness" is never ultimate. God never delights in sending his Son, for example, simply for its own sake. The sending of Christ
served an ultimate end—it is therefore a subordinate end. Likewise, the
church should never consider its being sent as ultimate; its sending is
subordinate to the preaching of the gospel, which itself is subordinate
to the creation of worshipers. Yet this backward thinking of "mission" as
ultimate, something valued for its own sake, is exactly what causes the
missional movement to place such a highly unbalanced emphasis upon
"incarnation" or "contextualization" to the neglect of what is truly ultimate. Mission is actually subordinate to everything else the church is and
does. The church is sent *so that* it can evangelize, make worshipers, and
shape Christians into the image of Christ.

Thus, the following is a clearer articulation of the relationship of worship and mission than that typically expressed or implied by missional
authors: (1) God's chief end is his own glory; (2) worship brings God ultimate glory, and thus creation of worshipers is the *missio Dei*; (3) although
redemption is an important purpose for God's mission, it is nevertheless
subordinate to the ultimate end of creating worshipers since God accom-

---

14. Michael Frost, "Michael Frost on Being the Missional Church (PGF 2007)," n.d., http://
www.youtube.com/watch?v=77ndCFSv47g; accessed December 22, 2012.

plishes his mission through redemption; (4) the *missio Dei* and the mission of the church are related, but not identical. The church's mission is to make disciples through the proclamation of God's Word so that they might draw near to communion with God through Christ by faith.

Authentic Worship

These conclusions help to clarify the biblical relationship between worship and mission. The second important relationship to determine in light of the missional philosophy of worship is of that between worship and culture. I have already evaluated several of the underlying assumptions of the missional view of culture. In particular, I drew several conclusions that will influence an understanding of how culture integrates with worship: (1) culture is the behavior of a people; (2) culture flows from religious commitments and worldview; and (3) cultural expressions are therefore not neutral and must be judged to discern what values formed them and whether they are compatible with Christianity and, more specifically, Christian worship. With these preliminary conclusions in mind, this section will evaluate several assumptions regarding the relationship between worship and culture articulated or implied by missional advocates.

One of the fundamental assumptions motivating the missional philosophy of contextualization in worship is an emphasis upon authenticity in worship. For example, Guder insists that "our changing cultural context also requires that we change our worship forms so that Christians shaped by late modernity can express their faith authentically and honestly."[15] Likewise, Stetzer and Putman argue that "worship must take on the expression that reflects the culture of the worshiper if it is to be authentic and make an impact."[16] Kimball insists, "since worship is about our expressing love and adoration to God, and leaders teaching people about God, then of course the culture will shape our expressions of worship."[17] This is important not only for the sake of the worshiper, however, since "one of the most effective evangelistic methods a church

15. Guder, *The Continuing Conversion of the Church*, 157.
16. Stetzer and Putman, *Breaking the Missional Code*, 100.
17. Kimball, "Emerging Worship," 298.

can use is exposing the unchurched to the authentic worship of God."[18] This requires a careful examination as to the nature of "authenticity" in worship and its relationship to cultural form.

What Is Authentic Worship?

The Merriam-Webster dictionary gives three basic definitions of "authentic" still in common use today:

1. not false or imitation: real, actual

2. true to one's own personality, spirit, or character

3. worthy of acceptance or belief as conforming to or based on fact[19]

If the definition missional authors use when arguing for authentic worship is the first, then this clearly falls in line with biblical emphasis. God does not desire worship that is false, fake, or disingenuous. In fact, this was what God condemned of the post-exilic Jews (Mal. 1) and the New Testament Pharisees (Matt. 15:8). God desires sincere worship (Heb. 10:22) that follows his commands. However, usually the second definition is implied when missional proponents advocate authentic worship today. In other words, in order for worship to be truly "authentic," people have to be real to themselves, often in reference to musical style. A person cannot worship, they argue, unless he can do so in styles that are his own—styles he is comfortable with and that are part of his culture and preferences.

There are several problems with this line of thinking. First, "authentic" expressions defined this way are often sinful. Since culture is human behavior, and all human behavior is moral (i.e., either good or evil), then the possibility that someone's "authentic" expression is sinful is quite real. Furthermore, since humans are completely depraved, there is always the

---

18. Stetzer, *Planting Missional Churches*, 263.
19. "authentic," *Merriam-Webster.com* (2011), http://www.merriam-webster.com; accessed January 24, 2013. The dictionary entry also includes an obsolete reference ("authoritative") and a reference in discussions of music theory ("of a church mode : ranging upward from the keynote; of a cadence: progressing from the dominant chord to the tonic"), neither of which are relevant to the present discussion. Also, the order of the entries as listed above has been deliberately altered in order to evaluate them in an inductive manner.

potential that the way a person naturally expresses himself could be sinful. The Bible teaches that every person is totally and completely depraved:

> The LORD saw that the wickedness of man was great in the earth, and that every intention of the thoughts of his heart was only evil continually. (Gen. 6:5)

> Now this I say and testify in the Lord, that you must no longer walk as the Gentiles do, in the futility of their minds. They are darkened in their understanding, alienated from the life of God because of the ignorance that is in them, due to their hardness of heart. They have become callous and have given themselves up to sensuality, greedy to practice every kind of impurity. (Eph. 4:17–19)

Both the will and understanding are corrupt:

> To the pure, all things are pure, but to the defiled and unbelieving, nothing is pure; but both their minds and their consciences are defiled. (Titus 1:15)

The natural man cannot do anything good, nor can he understand spiritual things:

> Jesus answered them, "Truly, truly, I say to you, everyone who commits sin is a slave to sin." (John 8:34)

> The natural person does not accept the things of the Spirit of God, for they are folly to him, and he is not able to understand them because they are spiritually discerned. (1 Cor. 2:14)

He does not and cannot seek God, nor does he desire to do so:

> As it is written: "None is righteous, no, not one; no one understands; no one seeks for God. All have turned aside; together they have become worthless; no one does good, not even one." "Their throat is an open grave; they use their tongues to deceive." "The

venom of asps is under their lips." "Their mouth is full of curses and bitterness." "Their feet are swift to shed blood; in their paths are ruin and misery, and the way of peace they have not known." "There is no fear of God before their eyes." (Rom. 3:10–18)

Thus man, left to himself, is completely depraved. Total depravity does not mean that man is as depraved as he could be, but that all of man is completely depraved. No part of man escapes the reach of depravity, not his will, not his actions, not his preferences, not his culture, and certainly not the way he communicates.

However, it is true that when arguing for authentic worship, missional authors are typically referring to believers. Thus they may insist that although unbelievers are totally depraved, believers have been changed, their desires have been renewed, and they have the Holy Spirit to lead them in their judgments and expressions. This is certainly the case. New creatures in Christ have been made new:

Therefore, if anyone is in Christ, he is a new creation. The old has passed away; behold, the new has come. (2 Cor. 5:17)

Christians are no longer slaves to sin:

But thanks be to God, that you who were once slaves of sin have become obedient from the heart to the standard of teaching to which you were committed, and, having been set free from sin, have become slaves of righteousness. (Rom. 6:17–18)

The Holy Spirit indwells them:

You, however, are not in the flesh but in the Spirit, if in fact the Spirit of God dwells in you. Anyone who does not have the Spirit of Christ does not belong to him. But if Christ is in you, although the body is dead because of sin, the Spirit is life because of righteousness. If the Spirit of him who raised Jesus from the dead dwells in you, he who raised Christ Jesus from the dead will also give life to your mortal bodies through his Spirit who dwells in you. (Rom. 8:9–11)

Nevertheless, although believers have been delivered from the penalty and power of sin, they have not yet been delivered from the presence of sin. Even believers still struggle every day with the influences of remaining depravity. Perhaps one of the strongest biblical examples of this is Paul's testimony in Romans 7:15–25:

> For I do not understand my own actions. For I do not do what I want, but I do the very thing I hate. Now if I do what I do not want, I agree with the law, that it is good. So now it is no longer I who do it, but sin that dwells within me. For I know that nothing good dwells in me, that is, in my flesh. For I have the desire to do what is right, but not the ability to carry it out. For I do not do the good I want, but the evil I do not want is what I keep on doing. Now if I do what I do not want, it is no longer I who do it, but sin that dwells within me. So I find it to be a law that when I want to do right, evil lies close at hand. For I delight in the law of God, in my inner being, but I see in my members another law waging war against the law of my mind and making me captive to the law of sin that dwells in my members. Wretched man that I am! Who will deliver me from this body of death? Thanks be to God through Jesus Christ our Lord! So then, I myself serve the law of God with my mind, but with my flesh I serve the law of sin.

Even believers cannot fully trust their own judgments and expressions without clear guidance from God. True, the Holy Spirit indwells believers, but he does not somehow magically lead them to right decisions. The Holy Spirit leads believers through his Word and by giving them wisdom to apply it rightly to their lives. Christians must study it and apply its teachings to every situation in their lives, and sometimes this will lead them to recognize that their "authentic expressions" are actually not pleasing to him.

The second problem with this missional emphasis on "authentic" worship as a defense for contextualization in worship is that acceptable worship is not natural; it must be learned. The missional philosophy assumes that right worship will come naturally to all Christians, that a new Christian will instinctively know how to worship, and therefore his natural impulses are the best guide. In fact, on this reasoning, unbelievers know how to worship as well; they only need to change their beliefs, which falls in line with an understanding of religion as simply a component of culture. Yet while it is true that Christians are new creatures with new hearts and new desires, ingrained habits, misguided assumptions, and remaining depravity prevent anyone from simply "knowing" how to worship. Many people assume that worship comes naturally—that people should just worship with whatever language is most comfortable to them. But if the Scriptures and church history reveal anything about worship, it is that left to themselves, even God's people will worship poorly. They must be taught to worship. This assumes, of course, that such a thing as "wrong worship" exists, a point which cultural relativists would deny. However, understanding culture as behavior and recognizing the possibility of unholy culture leads to the inevitable conclusion that some ways of behaving in worship, including cultural expressions like music, may be unholy and/ or inappropriate for the occasion.

Rather than focusing on personal preference as the ultimate standard of authentic worship, truly authentic worship is that which conforms to God's standards. This is reflected in the final dictionary entry for "authenticity":

> 3. worthy of acceptance or belief as conforming to or based on fact

Truly "authentic" worship is not that which is based on one's own natural instincts, "heart language," preferences, or even cultural context. Truly authentic Christian worship is that which conforms to a standard—the standard of God's Word, as demonstrated further below.

Corporate Worship as the Shaper of Behavior

Thus, raising "authenticity," defined as being true to one's self, as the ultimate standard for cultural expression in worship misses a deeper purpose of worship in the believer's life. Worship is not simply the natural expression of a Christian; corporate worship—the public acting out of the spiritual realities of drawing near to God through Christ by faith— actually helps to shape the behavior—the "culture"—of God's people. The indigenous cultural expressions are not automatically acceptable for Christian worship; in many cases the newfound faith of a people will require them to change their behavior, *especially* in their corporate worship. This is one of the purposes of ordered worship. Those with more Christian maturity structure worship in such a way that it shapes the affections and teaches others how to worship rightly.

Christians Are a New Ethnos United around New "Culture"

Rather than simply adopting the cultural expressions of the people around them, Christian churches form a new, distinct race that unites around a new way of behaving. In 1 Peter 2:9, Peter calls the church a holy nation (*ethnos*), here used metaphorically to describe the new people God has created in the church:

> But you are a chosen race, a royal priesthood, a holy nation, a people for his own possession, that you may proclaim the excellencies of him who called you out of darkness into his marvelous light. (1 Peter 2:9)

Hiebert explains:

> The term was also used at times of Israel as the people of God united by their covenantal relation to him, making them distinctly his nation. It is in that latter sense that Peter applied the term to the church, which forms a unique international nation having a common spiritual life from God and committed to his rule. *Holy* indicates its separation from the nations of the world and consecration to God and his service. Its position of separation demands that the members must not, like Israel of old, stoop to the sinful practices of the world (1 Peter 1:15–17).[20]

Chapter 5 argued that "nation" is not the same as "culture," but rather that a "nation" is a group of people that share a common way of behaving ("culture"). This behavior, according to 1 Peter 1:15, ought to be holy: "But as he who called you is holy, you also be holy in all your conduct." Christians are not supposed to be defined as indigenous residents of unbelieving communities; rather, they are to be "sojourners and exiles" (1 Peter 2:11; cf. 1

---

20. Hiebert, *First Peter*, 134. Emphasis original.

Peter 1:17). As explained in chapter 5, often the behavior of unbelievers will resemble the behavior of Christians (even behavior in public worship), but this is not because Christians mimic unbelievers; it is because unbelievers have borrowed Christian values in those particular behaviors.

New Creatures—New Culture

Therefore, since Christians have been "ransomed from the futile ways inherited from [their] forefathers," since their values and worldview are now different from when they were unbelievers, and since they are not members of a new and distinct *ethnos*, new Christians need to be taught how "to behave in the household of God" through the process of discipleship.

Public worship, consequently, is a significant means for teaching this new "culture." The liturgy, cultural forms chosen, and biblical content of a worship service help to shape and form believers into acceptable worshipers. Calvin Johansson explains this well:

> Though worship belongs to God, it has an effect upon the worshiper, determined largely by its quality and design. We plan it. We craft it. We execute it. As a result, this which we fashion, the work of our hands, molds us in its own image. Worship itself has an outcome which is directed back to the believer. Though not particularly self-evident, in large measure, worship determines the quality of our walk with God. If it is immature, then the congregation becomes immature. The shape of our worship shapes us.[21]

Worship, Culture, and Truth

Another of the fundamental assumptions beneath the practice of contextualization common in the conservative evangelical missional movement is the belief that content and form have no intrinsic connection and are therefore easily separable. These conservative missional advocates admirably repudiate emergent leaders who argue that both content and form must be contextualized; they insist that since God's Word is inspired and inerrant, God's truth transcends culture and must be preserved intact.

---

21. Calvin M. Johansson, *Discipling Music Ministry: Twenty-First Century Directions* (Peabody, MA: Hendrickson Publishers, 1992), 16–17.

But since they consider culture as entirely neutral in itself, the form in which Christians communicate truth is fully fluid. This is seen in Hesselgrave and Rommen's distinction between cultural contextualization that is "true to … indigenous culture" and theological contextualization that is "true to … the authority of Scripture."[22] They point out that the conservative evangelical adaptation of contextualization included a "sensitivity to context and a fidelity to Scripture."[23] Likewise, while Towns and Stetzer defend certain essential truths based on being "biblically faithful," they nevertheless argue that such truth must be "culturally relevant."[24] Parris specifically relates this to forms in worship, insisting that "worship style will vary in form" while the "biblical message will remain pure."[25]

What Is Truth?

This simplistic dichotomy fails to understand the nature of truth, however; form and content are not as separable as missional advocates insist. Pilate's question to Jesus in John 18:30—"What is truth?"—is no less relevant today than it was then. In its most basic definition, something is true if it corresponds with reality.[26] The truth of which the church is the pillar and support (1 Tim. 3:15) has been revealed through the written Word of God. Everything contained within God's Word corresponds rightly with reality, and it is the church's responsibility to pass that truth on to future generations (Acts 20:27). Therefore, the truth the church is tasked to communicate can be no less than doctrinal.

Yet the truth given through Scripture—what churches are charged with proclaiming—is more than brute theological facts compiled in abstract statements. This truth is no less than facts in statements to be sure, but it is more. Modernism has led Christianity to equate truth with factuality alone, but an essential part of truth exists beyond mere factual correspondence. The authority and sufficiency of Scripture demand this. The Bible does not come to God's people as a collection of propositional

---

22. Hesselgrave and Rommen, *Contextualization*, 55.
23. Ibid., 33.
24. Towns and Stetzer, *Perimeters of Light*, 13.
25. Parris, "Instituting a Missional Worship Style," 2.
26. This is called the correspondence theory of truth in contrast to other theories like the pragmatic or coherence theories. For a helpful summary and analysis of the various theories, see Chad V. Meister, "Truth, Evangelicalism, and the Bible," *Christian Apologetics* 5, no. 1 (2006): 107–22.

statements or a systematic theology. As Kevin Vanhoozer observes, "The Bible is more than divine data."[27] Instead, God's revelation of truth comes in various literary forms, most of which are not merely didactic or propositional. James S. Spiegel helpfully summarizes the various literary genres that God chose to communicate his truth:

> . . . the books of the Bible are, in the main, works of literary art. From Genesis to Revelation we find epic narratives (tragic and comic), proverbs, poems, hymns, oratory, and apocalyptic literature whose artistic tools include allegory, metaphor, symbolism, satire, and irony. Comparatively little of the biblical material is strictly didactic, and where this is the case, such as in the book of Romans, the logical rigor itself is elegant (an aesthetic quality). Finally, Jesus' own preferred method of instruction, the parable, is an aesthetic device. And even when not using parables, his language tends to be heavily laden with metaphors and symbolism, a fact that exasperated the disciples.[28]

These forms provide a way of communicating God's truth that would be impossible with systematic statements of fact alone. These aesthetic forms are essential to the truth itself since God's inspired Word is exactly the best way that truth could be presented. Clyde S. Kilby observes, "The Bible comes to us in an artistic form which is often sublime, rather than as a document of practical, expository prose, strict in outline like a textbook."[29] He asserts that these aesthetic forms are not merely decorative but part of the essential presentation of the Bible's truth:

> We do not have truth and beauty, or truth decorated with beauty, or truth illustrated by the beautiful phrase, or truth in a "beautiful setting." Truth and beauty are in the Scriptures, as indeed they must always be, an inseparable unity.[30]

---

27. Kevin J. Vanhoozer, *The Drama of Doctrine: A Canonical-Linguistic Approach to Christian Theology* (Louisville: Westminster John Knox Press, 2005), 5.
28. James S. Spiegel, "Aesthetics and Worship," *Southern Baptist Journal of Theology* 2, no. 4 (1998): 44.
29. Clyde S. Kilby, *Christianity and Aesthetics* (Chicago: Inter-Varsity Press, 1961), 19.
30. Ibid., 21.

To reduce God's truth, then, only to doctrinal statements divorced from form does great injustice to the way God himself has chosen to reveal truth to us. Vanhoozer articulates this well:

> There are other types of precision or clarity than the scientific. It has been said, for example, that poetry is "the best words put in the best order." Similarly, because we are dealing with the Bible as God's word, we have good reason to believe that the biblical words are the right words in the right order. . . .

> To interpret the Bible truly, then, we must do more than string together individual propositions like beads on a string. This takes us only as far as fortune cookie theology, to a practice of breaking open Scripture in order to find the message contained within. What gets lost in propositionalist interpretation are the circumstances of the statement, its poetic and affective elements, and even, then, a dimension of its truth. We do less than justice to Scripture if we preach and teach only its propositional content. Information alone is insufficient for spiritual formation. We need to get beyond "cheap inerrancy," beyond ascribing accolades to the Bible to understanding what the Bible is actually saying, beyond professing biblical truth to practicing it.[31]

This is not to say that God was somehow constrained by human cultural forms in his communication of truth. Yarnell addresses this:

> . . . the Word itself is not bound by languages but utilizes human languages for it purpose. Indeed, the Word stands in judgment of language even as it enters that language to transcend the limits of a particular culture and introduce the God who is above all culture.[32]

Rather, in the process of divine inspiration, God chose to reveal his truth using particular aesthetic forms. Most missional advocates, however, view

---

31. Kevin J. Vanhoozer, "Lost in Interpretation? Truth, Scripture, and Hermeneutics," *Journal of the Evangelical Theological Society* 48, no. 1 (2005): 96, 100.
32. Yarnell, "Global Choices," 21.

the Bible—and by extension truth—as merely propositional.[33] To most, whatever aesthetic aspects are present in Scripture are incidental at best and for many a distraction. Truth is simply something to believe and perhaps get excited about.

To be clear, this argument does not deny the propositional nature of truth. Truth can—and indeed often must—be summarized in propositional statements. The argument at present is that truth is more than mere propositions. Again, Vanhoozer explains:

> Without some propositional core, the church would lose its *raison d'être*, leaving only programs and pot-lucks. At the same time, to reduce the truth of Scripture to a set of propositions is unnecessarily reductionist. What the Bible as a whole is literally about is theodrama—the words and deeds of God on the stage of world history that climax in Jesus Christ.[34]

Nor is this argument for two kinds of truth, one propositional and the other not; the argument here is that truth is always both propositional and aesthetic.

Thus what churches are charged with communicating is not only a collection of propositions that correspond to God's reality but also ways of expressing these ideas that likewise correspond to God's reality. Churches are committed to proclaiming not just intellectual facts but "the faith that was once for all delivered to the saints" (Jude 1:3). Faith is more than facts; faith is right facts combined with the affection of trust; faith is right facts felt rightly.

Truth and the Moral Imagination

If truth is more than factual correspondence—if it has an aesthetic aspect to it—then both the apprehension and the presentation of truth involve more than just intellect; they involve the aesthetic part of man, in particular, his imagination. Today the term "imagination" is used to mean

---

33. For a helpful comparison between the typical evangelical view of the Bible and truth and one that sees the imagination as essential to truth, see Peter W. Macky, "The Role of Metaphor in Christian Thought and Experience as Understood by Gordon Clark and C. S. Lewis," *Journal of the Evangelical Theological Society* 24, no. 3 (1981): 238–50.

34. Vanhoozer, "Lost in Interpretation?," 100–101.

something more similar to "fiction." Yet the imagination is much more than the dreamer's fantasy or the lover's wish. Human imagination is the way in which we interpret facts and is thus the way in which we make sense of truth. Scottish poet and pastor George MacDonald explains:

> To inquire into what God has made is the main function of the imagination. It is aroused by facts, is nourished by facts, seeks for higher and yet higher laws in those facts; but refuses to regard science as the sole interpreter of nature, or the laws of science as the only region of discovery.[35]

If God's reality is more than just facts and therefore truth is more than mere factual accuracy, imagination is what allows people to perceive the part of truth that is beyond intellectual knowledge alone. As has been argued, truth is correspondence to reality, but there are different kinds of correspondence, not all of which are propositional. Sometimes non-propositional correspondence does a better job of helping navigate reality than does propositional correspondence. For example, an aerial photograph of Washington, DC is like propositional correspondence; it is an exact representation of the way things are. A map of DC, on the other hand, is like metaphorical correspondence; it corresponds to reality, but in a way that highlights and emphasizes certain aspects of that reality over others.

Perception and interpretation of truth depend upon imagination of that truth. Leland Ryken helpfully explains how imagination affects how people view truth and what they do with truth:

> It is a fallacy to think that one's worldview consists only of ideas. It is a world picture as well as a set of ideas. It includes images that may govern behavior even more than ideas do. At the level of ideas, for example, a person may know the goal of life is not to amass physical possessions. But if his mind is filled with images of fancy cars and expensive clothes and big houses, his behavior will likely follow a materialistic path. A person might say that God created the world, but if his mind is filled with images of evolutionary processes, he will start to

---

35. George MacDonald, *The Imagination, and Other Essays* (Boston: D. Lothrop, 1883), 3.

think like an evolutionist. Someone may know that he should eat moderately, but his appetites override that knowledge when his mind is filled with images of luscious food. The imagination is a leading ingredient in the way people view reality. They live under its sway, whether they realize it or not.[36]

Because of this reality, form and content are not so easily separable. In the words of media ecologist Marshall McLuhan, "the medium is the message."[37]

Imagination in the Bible. This is why the Bible uses tools of the imagination to communicate truth. It contains literary forms that utilize various aesthetic devices, not just to decorate truth or make it more interesting, but in order to rightly shape our imagination of truth. As Vanhoozer claims, "Indeed, the panoply of genres in the Bible is nothing less than the imagination in full literary display."[38] This reality reveals the essential importance of the imagination in the communication of truth:

The point is not simply that the Bible allows for the imagination as a form of communication. It is rather that the biblical writers and Jesus found it impossible to communicate the truth of God without using the resources of the imagination. The Bible does more than sanction the arts. It shows how indispensable they are.[39]

Perhaps a good illustration of this is with narratives, which comprise a majority of the Bible's content. Many view narratives in Scripture as merely summaries of historical facts, but Vanhoozer explains how narratives do much more:

Narratives allow storytellers to create a unified whole from a succession of events. To be sure, there are modern despisers of

36. Leland Ryken, "The Bible as Literature Part 4: 'With Many Such Parables': The Imagination as a Means of Grace," *Bibliotheca Sacra* 147, no. 587 (1990): 393.
37. Marshall McLuhan, *Understanding Media: The Extensions of Man* (New York: McGraw-Hill, 1964), 23.
38. Vanhoozer, *The Drama of Doctrine*, 278.
39. Ryken, "The Bible as Literature Part 4," 392–93.

narrative as there are despisers of metaphor; some see narrative as merely the rhetorical icing on historical discourse. The propositionalist temptation is to regard narrative simply as the pretty packaging of historical content to be torn off and discarded. But the point of narrative is not merely to assert "this happened, and then this happened." Narratives make another kind of claim altogether: "look at the world like this." Narratives do more than chronicle; they *configure*. Configuration is the act of grouping people and events together in a meaningful whole and is, as such, an act of the narrative imagination, a power of synoptic vision.

Narratives explain why a certain event happened by *emplotment*, not by adducing causal laws but by situating it in an intelligible story. Narrative is the form that a distinctly historical understanding takes: certain things concerning human temporality and teleology can *only* be said in the form of narrative. Like metaphors, narratives are irreducible to propositionalist paraphrase. Following a story requires a different cognitive skill than does following an argument, but it is no less cognitive for that.[40]

Imagining Truth. The point here is that if churches communicate propositional statements of truth alone in the form of systematic theology and doctrinal confession, and yet they have not preserved a biblically informed imagination of those facts, they have not succeeded in communicating the truth. So, for example, the "Young Messiah" is not a faithful communication of Handel's masterpiece, a Precious Moments depiction of Noah and the Ark is not an accurate communication of the biblical account, and Curtis Allen's rap version of the Heidelberg catechism is not a true representation of that historic confession.[41]

Commitment to the verbal, plenary inspiration of Scripture implies that God inspired the Bible's ideas, words, *and* forms, and this demands a commitment to expressing not just the ideas of truth expressed in the

---

40. Vanhoozer, *The Drama of Doctrine*, 282. Emphasis original.
41. http://www.sovereigngraceministries.org/blogs/sgm/post/Video-Curt-Allen-performing-his-Heidelberg-Catechism-rap-live.aspx; accessed November 29, 2012.

Bible but also the way those ideas are imagined through Scripture's various aesthetic forms.

Truth and Worship Forms

The argument to this point has been that communicating the truth must include not only the expression of right doctrine but also the expression of right imagination. The imagination is shaped and cultivated through aesthetic forms. The focus has been most specifically on literary forms since this is what exists in the Bible, but all art forms shape the imagination in some way. This leads to the next point of the argument, namely, that rightly ordered worship is essential to the preservation and communication of truth, for it is in worship that the imagination is most powerfully cultivated.

What art forms are chosen in worship is of utmost importance since they present to the congregation not just theological facts, but those facts imagined in certain ways. John Mason Hodges explains the power of worship forms in this regard:

> Our musical and liturgical choices in worship can display an aspect of God that is often ignored. We must ask ourselves, how can we whet the congregation's appetites now for the satisfactions that will be theirs in God for eternity? One way would be to commit ourselves to the pursuit of God's beauty made manifest through his creation and ours, and value that beauty highly when making decisions for worship.[42]

Most evangelicals today, including missional advocates, view worship forms as simply pretty packaging for truth or at best a way to "energize" the truth. Music is just a way to make truth interesting and engaging in worship. Stetzer reflects this when he suggests that the purpose of music in the context of worship is simply to "relieve anxiety and create interest for unbelievers who have not attended church for years."[43] But imaginative forms are not incidental to truth—they are essential to the truth, as Spiegel explains: "At its best, liturgical art is not merely consistent with

---

42. John Mason Hodges, "Aesthetics and the Place of Beauty in Worship," *Reformation and Revival* 9, no. 3 (2000): 73.
43. Stetzer, *Planting Missional Churches*, 265.

sound doctrine but serves positively to illuminate biblical teaching, making imaginative expression or application of biblical truth."[44]

Therefore, worship forms help to express the imaginative aspect of truth in ways that propositional statements alone cannot; they communicate not just the *what* of biblical content, but also *how* that content is imagined. Johansson explains why this is important, with special attention given to worship music:

> . . . the form of the instruction (as well as the content) must not work against the ultimate goal of the instruction—maturity in Christ. The best instructional forms are neither frivolous, irrelevant, nor trivial. If the aim is to mature the Christian, instruction should be designed in such a way that maturity results. Poorly crafted stories that use inappropriate language and faulty structure, or emphasize inconsequential points, may be fun for children, but they do not result in sound Christian education. Fashioning the form to match the goal will better insure its attainment. Any music used in teaching ought to help the student grow and develop. Music which is immature for people at a particular level of development does little for promoting growth.[45]

And the kinds of imaginative forms God chose to communicate his truth should inform churches' worship forms today. Art in worship is more than incidental; it is God-ordained because of its power to express rightly imagined truth: "Surely the fact that God himself chose an artistic medium as his primary vehicle of special revelation ought by itself to persuade us to place a special premium on the arts."[46]

Aesthetic form shapes propositional content; just like a liquid takes the shape of its container, doctrinal facts take the shape of the aesthetic form in which they are carried. This is accomplished in worship music through poetic devices and structural elements that work together to shape the content, such as cadences, tonality, tempo, meter, rhythm, dynamics, density, timbre, register, texture, and motivic development. The problem is that

---

44. Spiegel, "Aesthetics and Worship," 51.
45. Johansson, *Discipling Music Ministry*, 16.
46. Spiegel, "Aesthetics and Worship," 44.

since missional advocates understand truth to be only right knowledge of right facts, they view worship as a time to impart only right facts with some enjoyable music to make such transmission interesting or engaging. Yet while theological facts must be transmitted in worship, this misses the whole point of worship, as Bryan Chapell astutely observes:

> The negative impact of turning the sanctuary into the lecture hall is training believers to become merely reflective about the gospel in worship and tempting them to believe that right worship is simply about right thought. As a consequence, the worship focus becomes study, accumulating doctrinal knowledge, evaluating the Sermon, and critiquing the doctrinally imprecise. Congregational participation, mutual encouragement, heart engagement, expressions of grief for sin, and joyous thanksgiving may increasingly seem superfluous, or even demeaning.[47]

Thus most theologically conservative missional worship services are filled with good doctrinal teaching but worship forms that may not express an imagination of that truth that rightly reflects biblical imagination. They view the purpose of worship music as making truth "engaging" rather than its deeper purpose of shaping imagination in profound ways. With this view, it matters not what kind of music a church uses as long as it is "passionate" and resonates with the worshipers as "authentic."

Worship choices, then, are not merely about what is pleasing, authentic, or engaging; what forms churches choose for worship must be based on the criterion of whether or not they are true—whether or not they correspond to God's reality as it is communicated aesthetically in his Word.

---

47. Chapell, *Christ-Centered Worship*, 67.

chapter 10

FOR THUS SAYS THE LORD:

WHO REGULATES WORSHIP?

For thus says the LORD of hosts, the God of Israel:
Do not let your prophets and your diviners who are among you deceive you
and do not listen to the dreams that they dream,
for it is a lie that they are prophesying to you in my name;
I did not send them, declares the LORD.
Jeremiah 29:8–9

During the Hebrew captivity, prophets like Jeremiah provided instruction of the same sort of critical cultural discernment I am advocating in this book. God permitted his people to evaluate the culture of their captors and participate in some aspects of that culture as long as they did not contradict his law.

However, when it came to their worship, the Lord's instructions were far more strict. The Hebrews were required to follow the clear directives given in the Law, and they were not allowed to add anything beyond what they were told. In other words, there was a distinction for Israel between how they interacted with culture on a daily basis and what they did in their formal worship.

If there is a particular way to behave in the household of God (1 Tim. 3:15), and if the aesthetic forms of Scripture itself should inform expressions used in worship today (as argued above), it follows that Christian worship should be regulated by Scripture similarly to Israel rather than a simplistic motivation to "contextualize" to the surrounding culture. This perspective, commonly called the regulative principle of worship, has been traditionally practiced by Presbyterians and Baptists, and it is well articulated in the London Baptist Confession of 1698:

> But the acceptable way of worshipping the true God is instituted by himself, and so limited by his own revealed will, that he may not be worshipped according to the imaginations and devices of men, nor the suggestions of Satan, under any visible representations, or any other way not prescribed in the Holy Scriptures. (22:1)

John Fawcett (1740–1817) summarized this characteristically Baptist conviction:

> No acts of worship can properly be called holy, but such as the Almighty has enjoined. No man, nor any body of men have any authority to invent rites and ceremonies of worship; to change the ordinances which he has established; or to invent new ones. ... The divine word is the only safe directory in what relates to his own immediate service. The question is not what we may think becoming, decent or proper, but what our gracious Master has authorized as such. In matters of religion, nothing bears the stamp of holiness but what God has ordained.[1]

Three general ideas govern the regulative principle of worship that limits what we may include in worship to only what God has prescribed:

The Sufficiency of Scripture

Second Timothy 3:16–17 teaches that the Bible is sufficient as the rule of faith and practice.

---

1. John Fawcett, *The Holiness Which Becometh the House of the Lord* (Halifax: Holden and Dawson, 1808), 25.

> All Scripture is breathed out by God and profitable for teach-
> ing, for reproof, for correction, and for training in righteous-
> ness, that the man of God may be competent, equipped for
> every good work.

The doctrine of the sufficiency of Scripture teaches that

> Scripture contained all the words of God he intended for his
> people to have at each stage of redemptive history, and that it
> now contains all the words of God we need for salvation, for
> trusting him perfectly, and for obeying him perfectly.[2]

Certainly God would not leave the church without instruction in the most
important issue on earth—his worship. God has given churches in his Word
all the instruction they need to obey him perfectly in the area of worship.

This point alone, however, does not fully settle the matter. Many theological traditions agree that God has given the church everything it needs
in Scripture to worship him rightly; however, some argue that God's all-
sufficient Word does not give explicit instructions regarding worship, and
therefore by implication God has given churches freedom to worship as
they think best as long as it does not go against his commands. Thus, two
additional biblical points clarify the matter.

God Rejects Worship That He Has Not Prescribed

Throughout Scripture, both in the Old and New Testaments, examples abound of God rejecting (often violently) worship that includes
elements that he has not prescribed. Rarely are these elements introduced with malicious intent—usually the motive is to enhance the
worship of Yahweh. But God nevertheless rejects worship that includes
such extra-biblical elements.

A first example may be found during the giving of the Law at Sinai:

> When the people saw that Moses delayed to come down
> from the mountain, the people gathered themselves together

---

2. Wayne Grudem, *Systematic Theology* (Grand Rapids: Zondervan, 1995), 127.

to Aaron and said to him, "Up, make us gods who shall go before us. As for this Moses, the man who brought us up out of the land of Egypt, we do not know what has become of him." So Aaron said to them, "Take off the rings of gold that are in the ears of your wives, your sons, and your daughters, and bring them to me." So all the people took off the rings of gold that were in their ears and brought them to Aaron. And he received the gold from their hand and fashioned it with a graving tool and made a golden calf. And they said, "These are your gods, O Israel, who brought you up out of the land of Egypt!" When Aaron saw this, he built an altar before it. And Aaron made proclamation and said, "Tomorrow shall be a feast to the LORD." (Ex. 32:1–5)

People often assume that the children of Israel were attempting to worship a pagan god in this instance. However, closer examination will show that they were simply trying to worship Yahweh using means he had not prescribed. In verse 1 the people say, "Up, make us [*elohim*] . . ." The same term is used in verse 4 when they say, "These are [this is] [*elohim*], O Israel, who brought you up out of the land of Egypt!" Some translators render this word, *elohim*, as "gods" because it is a plural reference to deity and because they assume the people of Israel are seeking to worship other gods.[3] However, what Aaron says in verse 5 clarifies who they were attempting to worship: "Tomorrow shall be a feast to [*Yhwh*]." There is little doubt here that the people were attempting to worship Yahweh, who they say brought them up out of Egypt. The name *Elohim* is often used to refer to Yahweh. The plural form signifies majesty and honor. This point is made even clearer when Moses relates this incident in Deuteronomy 9:16:

> And I looked, and behold, you had sinned against the LORD your God. You had made yourselves a golden calf. You had turned aside quickly from the way that the LORD had commanded you.

---

3. Both the NASB and HCSB translators render these cases as singular, however. Additionally, the HCSB capitalizes *God* in verse 4, although it does not in verse 1.

Moses says that they sinned against *Yahweh Elohim*. And he severely punished them, not because they were attempting to worship another god, but rather, as Moses says, they had "turned aside quickly from the way that the LORD had commanded [them]." They had introduced elements into the worship of Yahweh that he had not prescribed. Durham reflects this view: "In demanding such an image, the people have violated, first of all, the second commandment."[4] This event

> is not an account of the abandonment of Yahweh for other gods; it is an account of the transfer of the center of authority of faith in Yahweh from Moses and the laws and symbols he has announced to a golden calf without laws and without any symbols beyond itself.[5]

A second example of God rejecting worship he had not prescribed may be found with the sons of the high priest Aaron:

> Now Nadab and Abihu, the sons of Aaron, each took his censer and put fire in it and laid incense on it and offered unauthorized fire before the LORD, which he had not commanded them. And fire came out from before the LORD and consumed them, and they died before the LORD. Then Moses said to Aaron, "This is what the LORD has said, 'Among those who are near me I will be sanctified, and before all the people I will be glorified.'" And Aaron held his peace. (Lev. 10:1–3)

In this passage Nadab and Abihu offer an unauthorized fire—literally a "strange" fire—to the Lord, and they were killed for it. There was nothing inherently evil or profane about what they were doing.[6] But the fact that, as verse one states, the Lord had not commanded this element of worship, they were killed. God is very serious about this; the only acceptable worship is that which he himself has commanded.

A third example may be found in New Testament concerning the Pharisees:

---

4. Durham, *Exodus*, 422.
5. Ibid., 421–22.
6. Cf. R. K. Harrison, *Leviticus* (Downers Grove, IL: InterVarsity, 1980), 109–10.

This people honors me with their lips, but their heart is far from me; in vain do they worship me, teaching as doctrines the commandments of men. (Matt. 15:8–9)

Here Jesus is scolding the Pharisees who have added their own ingenuity to worship, and they are requiring others to take part in these same worship elements that God has not prescribed. These added elements were not evil in and of themselves, but the fact that they are not commanded by God renders the worship vain.

What is clear from these few examples is that God rejects worship that is not based on his commands even when it is offered with good motives. This may seem to be a difficult and restrictive truth, but it is what Scripture teaches, as Calvin notes:

I know how difficult it is to persuade the world that God disapproves of all modes of worship not expressly sanctioned by his Word. The opposite persuasion which cleaves to them—being seated, as it were, in their very bones and marrow—is, that whatever they do has in itself a sufficient sanction, provided it exhibits some kind of zeal for the honor of God. But since God not only regards as fruitless, but also plainly abominates, whatever we undertake from zeal to his worship, if at variance with his command, what do we gain by a contrary course? The words of God are clear and distinct; 'Obedience is better than sacrifice.' And 'in vain do they worship me, teaching for doctrines the commandments of men.'[7]

Extent of the Church's Authority/Liberty of Conscience

The third principle is clearly laid out in the New Testament since some Christians insisted upon introducing Jewish worship elements into Christian worship—elements that had not been prescribed for church worship. Paul deals with this issue specifically in Romans 14.

---

7. John Calvin, *The Necessity of Reforming the Church*, trans. H. Beveridge (London: W. H. Dalton, 1843), 11.

> One person esteems one day as better than another, while
> another esteems all days alike. Each one should be fully con-
> vinced in his own mind. The one who observes the day, ob-
> serves it in honor of the Lord. The one who eats, eats in
> honor of the Lord, since he gives thanks to God, while the
> one who abstains, abstains in honor of the Lord and gives
> thanks to God. (Rom. 14:5–6)

In Romans 14, Paul is dealing specifically with those Christian Jews who
desired to maintain religious restrictions and observances from the Mosaic Law. The important thing to remember here is that these are religious
restrictions of ceremonially unclean (*koinon*) food and observances of sacred days. Any proper discussion of so-called "Christian liberty" in this
passage must be framed in this context. In other words, while 1 Corinthians 8–10 applies to general things with negative associations from the
pagan world like meat offered to idols, Romans 14 deals with the more
narrowed topic of adding requirements to religious life. So this passage
has direct application to the issue of public worship, and the formulators
of the regulative principle applied it that way.

Within a context of "[making] every effort to do what leads to peace
and to mutual edification" (v. 19), Paul insists in verse 5 that "each one
should be fully convinced in his own mind" concerning sacred days, and
in verse 23 he warns that "the man who has doubts is condemned if
he eats, because his eating is not from faith; and everything that does
not come from faith is sin." The question is, should Christians observe
sacred days that have not been prescribed for church worship? Paul argues that in order to institute something like that, each person must be
convinced in his own mind. One must be careful not to impose upon his
own conscience or the conscience of another that of which they are not
fully convinced. And what is the only way that Christians can be fully
convinced that God wants us to observe a particular sacred day? One will
be persuaded only if God has prescribed it for the church. If a particular
Christian as an individual is convinced for some reason that he should
observe it, then he has every right to do so in his home. But church leaders cannot extend such an observance to gatherings of the church where
they have dozens or hundreds of individual consciences that must be convinced from the Word of God that such observance is necessary.

Formulators of the regulative principle applied this to all the extra observances the churches (whether the Roman Catholic or Anglican) were adding to public worship. These church authorities had no right to do so because, since the New Testament did not prescribe them, every man could not be convinced that they were necessary. Delivuk summarizes their problem well:

> From the time of the vestments controversy of the latter six-teenth century, the Anglican additions to worship had given many sincere believers serious conscience problems. They believed that these innovations were not worship. Therefore, they had problems of conscience every time they participated in worship. A major goal of the Westminster Assembly was to protect believers with sensitive consciences.[8]

Therefore, the original purpose for the regulative principle was not to restrict unnecessarily corporate worship but to liberate stricken consciences from practices within corporate worship that were not expressly set forth in the Scriptures. They insisted that no man, including ecclesiastical authorities, had the right to constrain a worshiper to participate in an activity of worship that had no Scriptural directive. Gordon notes:

> The issue that gave birth to the regulative principle was the nature and limits of church power. The issue was not, for them, "worship" versus "the rest of life," but "those aspects of life governed by the church officers" versus those aspects of life not governed by the church officers.[9]

The contexts of both Romans 14 and the original formulation of the regulative principle demonstrate clearly a biblically warranted distinction between corporate worship and the rest of life, along with the regulative principle's particularly instructive application for the church—"In worship, the church is forbidden to add rites and ceremonies to those found in the Bible, because the conscience is to be free of human requirements."[10]

---

8. John Allen Delivuk, "Biblical Authority and the Proof of the Regulative Principle of Worship in The Westminster Confession," *Westminster Theological Journal* 58, no. 2 (Fall 1996): 242.
9. Gordon, "Some Answers about the Regulative Principle," 323.
10. Delivuk, "Biblical Authority," 242.

What is not commanded is forbidden. This is exactly how the London Baptist Confession (1689) frames the issue:

> God alone is Lord of the conscience, and hath left it free from the doctrines and commandments of men which are in any thing contrary to his Word, or not contained in it. So that to believe such doctrines, or obey such commands out of conscience, is to betray true liberty of conscience; and the requiring of an implicit faith, and absolute and blind obedience, is to destroy liberty of conscience and reason also. (22:2)

The matter of religious restrictions is also addressed in Colossians 2:20–23:

> If with Christ you died to the elemental spirits of the world, why, as if you were still alive in the world, do you submit to regulations—"Do not handle, Do not taste, Do not touch" (referring to things that all perish as they are used)—according to human precepts and teachings? These have indeed an appearance of wisdom in promoting self-made religion and asceticism and severity to the body, but they are of no value in stopping the indulgence of the flesh.

Here Paul is chiding Christians who are adding to their religious life elements that are merely requirements of men. Again, these "Do not handle, Do not taste, Do not touch" requirements are in the context of the church (vv 18–19) and have reference to specific religious restrictions carried over from the Mosaic Law. Paul is saying that for the sake of the unity of the Body, Christians must limit themselves to religious requirements that are clearly prescribed in the New Testament. He even argues that these restrictions do indeed have an appearance of wisdom and spirituality, but because they have not been commanded by God, they render the worship unacceptable to him. As Duncan notes, then,

> the key benefit of the regulative principle is that it helps to assure that God—not man—is the supreme authority for how corporate worship is to be conducted, by assuring that the Bi-

ble, God's own special revelation (and not our own opinions, tastes, likes, and theories), is the prime factor in our conduct of and approach to corporate worship.[11]

Regulation of Worship Elements and Forms

Thus what is clear is that public worship must be regulated by the Word of God. Ligon Duncan helpfully summarizes this regulative principle of worship:

> What is being argued here is that there must be scriptural warrant for all that we do [in public worship]. That warrant may come in the form of explicit directives, implicit requirements, the general principles of Scripture, positive commands, examples, and things derived from good and necessary consequences. These formulations of the Reformed approach to worship also acknowledge that lesser things about corporate worship may be decided in the absence of a specific biblical command but in accordance with faithful biblical Christian thinking under the influence of scriptural principles and sanctified reason and general revelation (e.g., whether to use bulletins, what time the services are to begin, how long they are to last, where to meet, what the ministers and congregation will wear, whether to use hymnals, how the singing is to be led, and the like). But the first things—the central elements, the principle parts, the essentials—have a positive warrant. The incidentals and accidentals will be guided by scriptural principles.[12]

Yet the question of whether cultural forms are essential or incidental often raises controversy even among proponents of the regulative principle. The discussion above, however, should shed light on the problem. As was explained earlier, Scripture itself comes from God in various literary forms, and therefore these inspired forms are authoritative as well.

---

11. Phillip Graham Ryken, Derek W. H. Thomas, and J. Ligon Duncan III, eds., *Give Praise to God: A Vision for Reforming Worship, Celebrating the Legacy of James Montgomery Boice* (Phillipsburg, NJ: P & R Publishing Company, 2011), 24.
12. Ibid., 23.

Therefore cultural expression is essential to the worship elements themselves and whether or not they faithfully comport to Scripture's teaching. What kinds of poetic expression and aesthetic forms God chose to use in the communication of his truth should inform and regulate the kinds of cultural expressions churches use as they communicate the gospel and disciple believers into acceptable worshipers of God.

This is important, because while there is certainly flexibility from time to time and civilization to civilization concerning what forms are used to communicate God's truth in worship, understanding the nature of cultural form leads to the conclusion that some forms are more suited to the communication of God's truth than others, and some forms may even do injustice to the truth when compared to the forms God chose to use in Scripture. For example, God chose to use the metaphor of shepherd to communicate certain truths about himself (e.g., Ps. 23), Christ (e.g., John 10:11), and elders within the church (e.g., 1 Peter 5:2). Someone, with noble motives of contextualizing these truths in civilizations where shepherding is not common, may choose the metaphor of a cattle-driver instead. Yet the images created by the idea of a cattle-driver are far different than that of a shepherd and thereby do not capture the imaginative import of the biblically inspired image. Additionally, significant change of form in worship from the kind of forms in Scripture may actually constitute the introduction of an entirely different element in worship than what has been prescribed. For example, when the approved element of preaching shifts in form from proclamation to conversation or dramatic recitation, the act has actually transformed into an entirely different element that God has not prescribed in Scripture.

The same is true for musical forms used in corporate worship. Although there are no musical scores in Scripture, and there is no mandate that worshipers today use the exact same musical idioms used, for example, in the Jewish temple, the aesthetic forms in Scripture, when properly studied and understood, do form boundaries and guidelines sufficient for the regulation of musical forms in corporate worship. This requires, of course, careful study of literary form in Scripture.[13] Additionally, the

---

13. Introductory study into the literary forms of Scripture include Robert Alter and Frank Kermode, eds., *The Literary Guide to the Bible* (Cambridge, MA: Harvard University Press, 1990); Leland Ryken and Tremper Longman, eds., *A Complete Literary Guide to the Bible* (Grand Rapids: Zondervan, 1993); Robert Alter, *The Art of Biblical Poetry* (Philadelphia: Basic Books, 2011); Robert Alter, *The Art of Biblical Narrative* (Philadelphia: Basic Books, 2011).

kinds of affections, moods, and sentiments expressed and promoted by Scripture in connection with worship, along with examples of corporate worship and the kinds of music used therein, should also regulate the kinds of musical expressions used in corporate worship.[14]

For the missional church, culture and contextualization define the framework for church ministry and worship. What this chapter has argued, however, is that Scripture—not culture—should govern, regulate, and shape corporate worship. This is true of both the content of worship and the aesthetic forms used to express that content. Since the Bible comes to us from God as inspired content *and* form, Scripture should govern both aspects of corporate worship. Both will certainly need translation and/or explanation from the original to the present, but translation sets the Scripture as the starting point, while typical "contextualization" begins by allowing the constructs to be governed by the culture.

---

14. Although it is beyond the scope of this book to explore this issue fully, see my *Worship in Song: A Biblical Approach to Music and Worship* (Winona Lake, IL: BMH Books, 2009) for a more thorough discussion.

chapter 11

THE LORD'S SONG IN A

FOREIGN LAND

How shall we sing the LORD's song
in a foreign land?
If I forget you, O Jerusalem,
let my right hand forget its skill!
Let my tongue stick to the roof of my mouth,
if I do not remember you,
if I do not set Jerusalem
above my highest joy!
Psalm 137:4–6

Christians today live in a strange land, just like Israel in captivity. Christians today wrestle with how they should relate to the culture of unbelievers around them, just like the Hebrews did. And Christians today often fail to worship God according to his Word in the name of "contextualizing" to their surroundings, similarly to Israel's persistent syncretism.

I have presented what I believe is the most biblical approach to the current cultural condition by analyzing the philosophy and practice of worship that has become perhaps most influential in evangelicalism, the conservative evangelical missional church movement. Although the movement has contributed positively to evangelicalism in many ways, including its strong emphasis upon fervent evangelism and its recognition of cultural shifts in the West, I have nevertheless argued that deficiencies in its understanding of the nature of culture, the posture of contextualization, and the relationship between worship and mission leaves the missional philosophy of worship without clear biblical and theological support and, ironically, renders it less able to accomplish God's mission for the church. I have insisted, rather, that God's mission is to create worshipers for his own glory; he accomplishes this mission through redemption, and he has tasked the church with making disciples who will worship him acceptably. This requires that churches communicate God's truth to both believers and unbelievers using cultural expressions that fittingly shape the content in similar ways that the Bible itself does. Only with this understanding will churches accomplish the mission God has given them for his glory.

In this concluding chapter, I'd like to briefly summarize my argument and then offer some practical applications and conclusions from the discussion.

The overarching principles of the missional church movement—missionary imperative, twenty-first-century western postmodernism as missionary context, and the incarnational mode of mission—shape the movement's philosophy and practice of worship. Since everything about the church's existence falls under the category of "mission," even public worship serves mission. Missional church advocates are critical of both the "attractional" worship model of the church growth movement as well as the "Inside & Out" model in which worship serves to motivate individual Christians to evangelize outside the church's walls. Rather, missional authors typically advocate for a model of worship that aims for it to be both an authentic expression of believers and a culturally relevant and "comprehensible" presentation for unbelievers.

According to missional authors, in order for worship to be authentic for believers and understandable for unbelievers, churches must evaluate their cultural context and contextualize worship to that culture. Since the West is post-Christendom culturally, churches must avoid allowing their worship to be shaped by forms nurtured during Christendom and instead shape their worship according to the cultural expressions most dominant in their target culture. This particular posture of contextualization is driven by the principle of incarnation, which suggests that as the

Son of God became incarnate in order to redeem the world, so churches must become incarnate in their cultures in order to reach those cultures, and this includes their worship forms.

The missional philosophy of worship is rooted in specific understandings of culture and contextualization. As I have shown, the current missional/evangelical definitions of culture find their substance in anthropological discourse, and thus the implications and applications that naturally flow from secular anthropology also find their way into the thinking and practice of missional evangelicals. This is particularly true with the anthropological understanding of culture as neutral and the related issue of religious beliefs being but one component of the broader idea of culture. I have shown how missional advocates accept these principles since the concept of culture comes through the discipline of anthropology in the first place.

I have also sought to place missional ideas of contextualization in a standard historical framework. After showing that, like culture, contextualization is a relatively novel idea developed in recent liberal-leaning missions conversations, the chapter explained how conservative evangelicals—including those of the missional bent—adopted the idea with reference to cultural form while nevertheless protecting the authority of Scripture by insisting that truth must never change regardless of culture. The chapter then surveyed the historic approaches toward culture that various Christian groups have articulated and demonstrated that the missional approach fits perfectly within the transformationalist framework.

I critiqued these positions along with articulating alternate views on a number of issues. First, I demonstrated that although the New Testament does not speak of "culture" *per se*, the idea of "behavior"—represented by terms like *anastrophe*—quite closely resembles the anthropological/missional definition of culture, taken on its own merits. While the standard definition of culture may be accepted in Christian discourse, however, the implications and applications typical to anthropological/missional discussions may not be accepted. Culture, defined as behavior, is clearly *not* neutral. All human behavior is moral, and therefore what is commonly called "culture" is either good or evil. Furthermore, religious belief is not just one part of culture, it is the pervading system from which culture ("behavior") flows. What a group or civilization believes concerning God, the world, humankind, and sin acts as the environment in which behavioral patterns are cultivated and out of which cultural forms emerge. Therefore Christians must evaluate all cultural expressions—especially those used in public worship—to determine what values and beliefs are embedded in those expressions and whether they are compatible with Christianity and corporate worship.

Presenting this reorientation with regard to culture and contextualization sets the stage for a more biblical understanding of worship, mission, and their relationship to each other. I explored the relationship between worship and mission by first defining worship biblically. It argued that the basic elements of worship, including communion in God's presence, sanctuary, priests, and atonement, were instituted in the creation/fall events, permeate the storyline of Scripture and culminate in the gospel of Jesus Christ, leading to a definition of worship as drawing near in communion with God through Christ by faith. This understanding of worship reveals the important connection between Christian worship and the gospel; redemption in Christ enables people to worship. I then discussed the significance of public worship. Contrary to missional authors, who suggest that little significant distinction exists between corporate worship and worship as Christian living, Scripture presents corporate worship as a sacred event in which the gospel is publicly acted out in order to strengthen the faith of believers and proclaim that gospel to unbelievers who may attend.

With this understanding in mind, I then continued by defining the mission of God, the mission of the church, and the relationship between this mission and worship. God's chief end is his own glory, his mission is the creation of worshipers, and he accomplishes the creation of worshipers through redemption. God's mission and the church's mission are related, but not the same, however. The church's mission, as articulated by passages like Matthew 28:18–20, is to make disciples. An initial step in this mission is the proclamation of the gospel, but that is not the full extent of what the church is tasked to do. Furthermore, although redemption is a primary task of God toward the end of creating worshipers, the church is never commanded to redeem anything; rather, the church makes disciples by proclaiming the gospel to individuals and teaching them God's commandments. Thus in making disciples, churches do participate in the mission of God to create a people who will draw near to communion with him through Christ by faith and thereby bring him ultimate glory.

Recognizing this relationship between worship and mission, I explored the issue of cultural forms within the context of corporate worship.

Contrary to the conservative evangelical missional position, which tries to artificially separate form and content when discussing worship expressions, the chapter argued that since aesthetic form shapes content, form is essential to the content itself. Therefore, as churches seek to communicate God's truth in corporate worship for the sake of making disciples and nurturing worshipers, they must ascertain which cultural forms best express and support that truth. The best way to accomplish this objective is to rely on the authority of Scripture, not only in articulating doctrine in propositional constructs, but also by the way in which that doctrine is expressed aesthetically.

This led to the final primary argument of the book, namely, that the Word of God should regulate corporate worship in its doctrinal content, liturgical elements, and the cultural forms used to express that doctrine in the liturgical context. I presented three primary arguments in favor of the regulative principle of worship, including the sufficiency of Scripture, the fact that in Scripture God rejects worship that he has not prescribed, and the limits of church authority on the free consciences of God's people. The last chapter concluded by extending the typical discussions of the regulative principle to cultural forms in worship, taking into consideration the earlier discussion of the authority of aesthetic form in Scripture.

Thus the book has argued that the most missional worship is that which seeks to glorify God in making disciple-worshipers by communicating God's truth through the use of appropriate cultural forms that are regulated by Scripture.

Implications and Applications

Ultimately, this book is not meant to address very specific application; rather, I have sought to lay the biblical groundwork that will allow church leaders to make informed, practical decisions regarding the relationship between worship and culture as they seek to reach an increasingly pagan culture. However, I will draw several general conclusions and applications from the arguments I have presented.

Christians should resist equating culture with race. As I have suggested, the idea most likely associated with culture today is "race," and any attempt to critically evaluate a particular cultural expression is, therefore, judged as racism. Yet as this book has demonstrated, race and culture are not equal. A race describes a group of people with shared ancestral and genetic roots, while culture describes behavior. Such behavior may be passed down through the traditions of a given race, but there is nothing inherently ethnic about any cultural expression. If Christian discussion regarding culture is going to move forward, especially as it relates to worship and evangelism, this misplaced connection must be rectified.

Churches should not start with the surrounding culture when choosing worship forms; they should start with Scripture. So much of the missional contextualization posture finds its starting point in analyzing and appropriating whatever cultural expressions dominate the surrounding society. Yet this framework sets the culture as the authority in church practice. Instead, churches should begin with the authoritative Word of God, seeking to develop a unique and holy culture that flows from biblical values. A certain amount of translation may be necessary to communicate those values and behavior to people who do not share the same constructs, but even the translation must accurately reflect Scripture. In some cases, the target audience may be so foreign to a biblical system of values that nothing about their indigenous culture is usable; in those cases church leaders will find it necessary to explain to them the meaning of holy cultural forms and teach them to learn to appreciate those kinds of forms.

For this reason, church leaders, and indeed all Christians, must have a skilled knowledge of the cultural forms used in the Bible to express its truth. A certain amount of study of biblical literary forms, including how they shape their content, will help a church leader better discern which forms in his culture best communicate truth. Likewise, church leaders should study the kinds of sentiments and affections the Bible prescribes for worship and choose worship forms that accurately express those affections.

This will also require that church leaders know how to parse the meanings and values of the cultural expressions within their own culture to determine whether or not they are compatible with Christian sentiments. This may be one area where the missional church emphasis is helpful—churches must know how the people in their community think and the worldviews that influence their thinking as well as how this thinking and worldview is embodied in their cultural expressions. Christians do not necessarily need to immerse themselves in the culture of their community in order for this to take place—in fact, that might sometimes be dangerous for one's spiritual well-being.

Corporate worship should make disciples. Disciple-making is the church's mission, and corporate worship must fit into this framework. Indeed, as I argued, making disciples and making worshipers are actually two aspects of the same mission. Thus, worship is not primarily about evangelism, nor is it an entirely vertical encounter. Corporate worship must contribute to the goal of making disciples so that they might worship God acceptably by leading people to draw near to communion with God through Christ by faith using appropriate cultural expressions.

This may be accomplished in public worship in at least three ways. First, corporate worship can proclaim the gospel in its very structure and content. Since corporate worship is the public acting out of the gospel—drawing near to God through Christ by faith—a liturgy structured to reflect that progression will both strengthen the believer and proclaim gospel truth to the unbeliever. Appropriating a structure such as that suggested in Chapell's *Christ-Centered Worship* ensures that true worship takes place and that unbelievers are always confronted with the gospel message when they attend a service. Likewise, the content of particular elements within the service, because they are chosen to fit specific moments in the gospel progression, also help to proclaim the gospel to believers and unbelievers alike.

Second, if worship is to make disciples it must contain rich, doctrinal content. Corporate worship is not simply about "authentic," "natural" expression of praise to God—it is about shaping people into disciple-worshipers. This means that teaching and preaching must be central in worship services, and the textual content of music must contribute to shaping people, both intellectually and spiritually, into worshipers for the glory of God.

Third, the aesthetic forms used to express that truth in corporate worship must be compatible with the content, for it, too, shapes the worshiper. Since form and content are not so easily divorced, and since the Bible's authority extends not just from its propositional truth but also from how that truth is expressed, there are limits as to what kinds of cultural forms are appropriate for use in corporate worship. Only those forms that shape their content in ways similar to the forms of Scripture may be used.

Churches should rely on the Judeo-Christian worship tradition. If churches are intent upon preserving and communicating the truth handed down from Scripture, both the truth's doctrinal content and the way it is imagined, they would be wise to continue preserving and cultivating what might be called the Judeo-Christian tradition. Churches have at their fingertips a rich heritage of cultural forms that have grown within the biblical value systems of Judaism and the historic Christian Church—forms that were cultivated with the goal of expressing transcendent biblical values. Although the church/state alliance of the Christendom period was ill-advised for many reasons and caused serious theological and ecclesiastical problems, by the providence of God it did create a tradition that perpetuated and cultivated worship forms of the same character as the biblical forms. The forms through the early nineteenth century were text-driven, modest, and distinguishable from the pagan culture; those with Bible-informed imaginations nurtured them in order to communicate that imagination to others.[1]

This cultivation of the Judeo-Christian worship tradition continued until revivalists in the early nineteenth century rejected the tradition in favor of the novelty and "excitement" of pop culture—they were among the first in church history to allow outside culture to shape the culture of worship. William McLoughlin observes that "[Charles G.] Finney's revivalism broke the dam maintained by 'The Tradition of the Elders' (the title of one of his most pungent sermons) and transformed 'the new system' from a minority to a majority religion."[2] From that point on, most of the evangelical movement has failed to cultivate this tradition but has instead favored more novel and "stimulating" cultural forms nurtured by secular culture. The Church is now ruled by what Loren Mead called the "Tyranny of the New"—a complete rejection of the Judeo-Christian tradition. Mead explains the problem with this rejection: "When the new way is considered the only way, there is no continuity, fads become the new Gospel and in Paul's words, the church is 'blown to and fro by every wind of

---

1. Space does not allow the full explanation of the development of the Judeo-Christian worship tradition or full support of these claims. For a more thorough exploration, see Quentin Faulkner, *Wiser Than Despair: The Evolution of Ideas in the Relationship of Music and the Christian Church*, 2nd ed. (Simpsonville, SC: Religious Affections Ministries, 2012); Stapert, *New Song for an Old World*.

2. William G. McLoughlin, *Modern Revivalism: Charles Grandison Finney to Billy Graham* (New York: Ronald Press, 1958), 66.

doctrine.'"[3] Quentin Faulkner devastatingly summarizes the effect of this rejection of tradition upon the worship of the Christian Church:

> Music (for that matter, all the arts) had become a theologi-
> cal orphan. In fact, no important theological movement, either
> in the nineteenth or twentieth century, has concerned itself in
> any profound way with the significance of harmony, order, or
> beauty in Christian life or [worship].[4]

Tradition is neither infallible nor authoritative in itself, but failure to preserve and accurately communicate God's truth, in both its doctrinal and aesthetic faithfulness to the revelation of God's Word, is due in large part to a failure to cultivate the Judeo-Christian worship tradition. In evangelicalism's desire to preserve and communicate the truth, churches must realize that they cannot start from nothing; since fully orbed truth is preserved and communicated in large part through worship forms, churches must be committed to preserving and nurturing those forms that have been cultivated within the Judeo-Christian tradition.

Churches should actively pass on their worship culture to their children. Since acceptable worship is something to be learned, churches should commit to teaching worship to their children at early ages. Unfortunately, most Christians do not recognize that before a child can even comprehend facts, his affections and imagination are already being shaped. In fact, most Christians never really even consider the moral imaginations of their children. They may be targeting their hearts, and by teaching them biblical doctrine their hearts are certainly influenced. But many churches fail to realize that a child's imagination is shaped long before he or she has the capacity to comprehend doctrinal facts. In other words, long before a child can comprehend his need to love the one true and living God, before he or she can comprehend the concept of a god at all, the child learns how to love. Long before a child can comprehend his need to fear and reverence God, the child learns how to fear and reverence. Long before a child can comprehend his purpose to worship God, the child learns how to worship.

---

3. Mead, *The Once and Future Church*, 11.
4. Faulkner, *Wiser Than Despair*, 190.

What happens with most churches, though, that see only the need to teach their children's minds, is that in order to teach such truths, they are willing to use almost whatever means necessary to do so. So they use puppets to teach Bible stories, never realizing that their children's imaginations are being shaped to view biblical truth as something light and trivial. They use cartoons to teach moral lessons, never realizing that their children's imaginations are being shaped to view morality as something silly or "adventurous." This problem occurs acutely in children's music. Christian parents, educators, and publishers have the noble goal of teaching their children about God, his Word, and how to obey him rightly, but they set such truth to irreverent, trivial music, forgetting that long before their children learn those doctrines, they must learn how to imagine those truths rightly.

Children learn to worship God primarily through participating in rightly ordered worship. Children learn to love God by first learning how to love. Children learn to reverence God by first learning how to reverence. Children learn to fear God by first learning how to fear. If evangelicalism fails to preserve and accurately communicate the truth, both in its factual and aesthetic correspondence to God's reality, it will be due in large part to its failure to shape their children's imaginations in their desire to teach them the truth.

Churches should actively cultivate evangelistic outreach outside the walls of the church building. While I have argued that the primary purpose of corporate worship is not evangelism, evangelism *is* the first step in accomplishing the church's mission of making disciples. And while even public worship can aid in that evangelism through its structure and content, making disciples of all nations will require that individual Christians fervently proclaim the gospel outside the normal meetings of the church.

Unfortunately, for a number of reasons, some of which are helpfully identified by the missional church movement, many Christians today view evangelism as little more than inviting unbelieving friends to a church service. For this reason, church leaders must actively encourage the people in their congregations to change this mindset and strategically plan ways to reach people with the gospel at other times. The missional church movement may be right that churches today are ineffective in evangelism. The answer is not to reduce corporate worship to weekly evangelistic events. The answer is to encourage regular, relational evangelism in the community.

Churches should consider themselves strangers and aliens in the world. Ultimately, the church's relationship to the surrounding culture is very similar to Israel in exile or the early church in its Greco-Roman environment. The missional church is correct that Christendom lulled the church into complacency. But the missional church falls prey to its own critique when it does not recognize the nature of post-Christendom as essentially hostile to Christianity. Churches today should relate to their surrounding situation in ways similar to the Hebrews in exile or the early church. They should be initially suspicious of any of the world's culture since in most cases the safe assumption is that the culture is an expression of unbiblical values. However, with that as the initial posture, Christians can be free to appropriate whatever culture happens to be, by God's common grace, an expression of a biblical worldview.

Conclusion

God has a mission, and that mission is to create a people who will draw near to communion with him by faith through the means that he has provided in the sacrificial atonement of his Son. As part of that mission, God has tasked the New Testament Church to help make disciple-worshipers through the proclamation of the gospel and teaching of his commandments. Corporate worship helps accomplish this mission, not by attracting unbelievers through "relevant" services or even through "contextualizing" the gospel message in cultural forms that are most appealing to unbelievers. Rather, corporate worship accomplishes the mission of God by being what it is—worship; the most missional worship is that which acts out the gospel and communicates God's truth using forms that are regulated by the authority of the Word of God.

If churches would return to this kind of corporate worship, they might see more examples of what Paul hoped for the Corinthian church when an unbeliever witnessed their worship:

> He is convicted by all, he is called to account by all, the secrets of his heart are disclosed, and so, falling on his face, he will worship God and declare that God is really among you. (1 Cor. 14:24–25)

BIBLIOGRAPHY

Alter, Robert. *The Art of Biblical Narrative*. Philadelphia: Basic Books, 2011.

_____. *The Art of Biblical Poetry*. Philadelphia: Basic Books, 2011.

Alter, Robert, and Frank Kermode, eds. *The Literary Guide to the Bible*. Cambridge: Harvard University Press, 1990.

Aniol, Scott. *Sound Worship: A Guide to Making Musical Choices in a Noisy World*. Simpsonville, SC: Religious Affections Ministries, 2010.

_____. *Worship in Song: A Biblical Approach to Music and Worship*. Winona Lake, IL: BMH Books, 2009.

Arnold, Matthew. *Culture and Anarchy: An Essay in Political and Social Criticism*. London: Smith, Elder, and Co, 1869.

Augustine. *City of God*. Translated by Marcus Dods. New York: The Modern Library, 1950.

Bahnsen, Greg L. *Pushing the Antithesis: The Apologetic Methodology of Greg L. Bahnsen*. Powder Springs, GA: American Vision, 2007.

Barth, Karl. *The Doctrine of God*. Edited by G. W. Bromiley and T. F. Torrance. Translated by T. H. L Parker, W. B. Johnston, Harold Knight, and J. L. M. Haire. Vol. 2. Church Dogmatics. Edinburgh: T&T Clark, 1957.

_____. *The Doctrine of Reconciliation*. Edited by G. W. Bromiley and T. F. Torrance. Translated by G. W. Bromiley. Vol. 4. Church Dogmatics. Edinburgh: T&T Clark, 1958.

_____. *The Knowledge of God and the Service of God According to the Teaching of the Reformation*. Translated by J. L. M. Haire and Ian Henderson. London: Hodder and Stoughton, 1938.

Begbie, Jeremy S. "Creation, Christ, and Culture in Dutch Neo-Calvinism." In *Christ in Our Place: The Humanity of God in Christ for the Reconciliation of the World: Essays Presented to Professor James Torrance*, edited by Daniel P. Thimell and Trevor A. Hart, 113–32. Allison Park, PA: Pickwick, 1989.

Black, Kathy. *Culturally-Conscious Worship*. St. Louis: Chalice Press, 2000.

Boas, Franz. "The History of Anthropology." In *A Franz Boas Reader: The Shaping of American Anthropology, 1883-1911*, edited by George W. Stocking, Jr., 23–35. Chicago: The University of Chicago Press, 1989.

Bock, Darrell L. *Acts*. Grand Rapids: Baker Academic, 2007.

Bosch, David. *Transforming Mission: Paradigm Shifts in Theology of Mission*. Maryknoll, NY: Orbis Books, 1991.

Brown, Colin, ed. *New International Dictionary of New Testament Theology*. Vol. 1. Grand Rapids: Zondervan, 1986.

Bullinger, Ethelbert William. *A Critical Lexicon and Concordance to the English and Greek New Testament: Together with an Index of Greek Words, and Several Appendices*. London: Longmans Green, 1908.

Bush, Perry. *Two Kingdoms, Two Loyalties: Mennonite Pacifism in Modern America*. Baltimore: The Johns Hopkins University Press, 1998.

Calvin, John. *Institutes of the Christian Religion*. Philadelphia: Westminster John Knox Press, 1960.

_____. *The Necessity of Reforming the Church*. Translated by H. Beveridge. London: W. H. Dalton, 1843.

Carson, D. A. *Christ and Culture Revisited*. Grand Rapids: Wm. B. Eerdmans, 2008.

Chapell, Bryan. *Christ-Centered Worship: Letting the Gospel Shape Our Practice*. Grand Rapids: Baker Academic, 2009.

Clement of Alexandria. *Miscellanies*. Vol. 2. Ante-Nicene Fathers. Grand Rapids: Wm. B. Eerdmans, 1986.

_____. *The Instructor*. Vol. 2. Ante-Nicene Fathers. Grand Rapids: Wm. B. Eerdmans, 1986.

Colijn, Brenda B. "'Let Us Approach': Soteriology in the Epistle to the Hebrews." *Journal of the Evangelical Theological Society* 39, no. 4 (December 1996): 570–86.

Couch, Mal. *A Bible Handbook to the Acts of the Apostles*. Grand Rapids: Kregel Academic, 2004.

Crouch, Andy. *Culture Making: Recovering Our Creative Calling*. Downers Grove, IL: InterVarsity Press, 2008.

Delivuk, John Allen. "Biblical Authority and the Proof of the Regulative Principle of Worship in The Westminster Confession." *Westminster Theological Journal* 58, no. 2 (Fall 1996): 235–56.

DeYoung, Kevin, and Greg Gilbert. *What Is the Mission of the Church? Making Sense of Social Justice, Shalom, and the Great Commission*. Wheaton, IL: Crossway, 2011.

Dooyeweerd, Herman. *Roots of Western Culture*. Toronto: Wedge, 1979.

Doran, David M. *For the Sake of His Name: Challenging a New Generation for World Missions*. Allen Park, MI: Student Global Impact, 2002.

Driscoll, Mark. *Confessions of a Reformission Rev.: Hard Lessons from an Emerging Missional Church*. Grand Rapids: Zondervan, 2009.

_____. *Religion Saves: And Nine Other Misconceptions*. Wheaton, IL: Crossway, 2009.

_____. *The Radical Reformission: Reaching Out without Selling Out*. Grand Rapids: Zondervan, 2006.

Driscoll, Mark, and Gerry Breshears. *Vintage Church: Timeless Truths and Timely Methods*. Wheaton, IL: Crossway, 2008.

DuBose, Francis. *God Who Sends: A Fresh Quest for Biblical Mission*. Nashville: Broadman Press, 1983.

Durham, John I. *Exodus*. Waco, TX: Word Books, 1987.

Dyck, Cornelius J. *An Introduction to Mennonite History: A Popular History of the Anabaptists and the Mennonites*. Scottdale, PA: Herald Press, 1981.

Eusebius. *Ecclesiastical History*. Translated by Roy J. Deferrari. Vol. 29. The Fathers of the Church. New York: Fathers of the Church, 1955.

Faulkner, Quentin. *Wiser Than Despair: The Evolution of Ideas in the Relationship of Music and the Christian Church*. 2nd ed. Simpsonville, SC: Religious Affections Ministries, 2012.

Fawcett, John. *The Holiness Which Becometh the House of the Lord*. Halifax: Holden and Dawson, 1808.

Frame, John. *The Escondido Theology: A Reformed Response to Two Kingdom Theology*. Lakeland, FL: Whitefield Media Productions, 2011.

Frost, Michael. "Michael Frost on Being the Missional Church (PGF 2007)," n.d. http://www.youtube.com/watch?v=77ndCFSv47g.

Gaebelein, Frank E., ed. *The Expositor's Bible Commentary, Volume 12: Hebrews through Revelation*. Grand Rapids: Zondervan Publishing House, 1981.

_____, ed. *The Expositor's Bible Commentary, Volume 8: Matthew, Mark, Luke*. Grand Rapids: Zondervan Publishing House, 1984.

Goheen, Michael. "'As The Father Has Sent Me, I Am Sending You': Lesslie Newbigin's Missionary Ecclesiology." PhD diss., Utrecht University, 2002.

_____. "Is Lesslie Newbigin's Model of Contextualization Anticultural?" *Mission Studies* 19, no. 1/2 (January 1, 2002): 136–56.

Goheen, Michael, and Albert M. Wolters. "Worldview between Story and Mission." In *Creation Regained: Biblical Basics for a Reformational Worldview*, by Albert M. Wolters. 2nd ed. Grand Rapids: Wm. B. Eerdmans, 2005.

Goodall, Norman, ed. *Missions Under the Cross: Addresses Delivered at the Enlarged Meeting of the Committee of the International Missionary Council at Willingen, in Germany, 1952; with Statements Issued by the Meeting*. London: Edinburgh House Press, 1953.

Gordon, T. David. "Some Answers about the Regulative Principle." *Westminster Theological Journal* 55, no. 2 (Fall 1993): 320–29.

Grudem, Wayne. *Systematic Theology*. Grand Rapids: Zondervan, 1995.

Guder, Darrell. *Missional Church: A Vision for the Sending of the Church in North America*. Grand Rapids: Wm. B. Eerdmans, 1998.

_____. *The Continuing Conversion of the Church*. Grand Rapids: Wm. B. Eerdmans, 2000.

Harrison, R. K. *Leviticus*. Downers Grove, IL: InterVarsity, 1980.

Hesselgrave, David J., and Edward Rommen. *Contextualization: Meanings, Methods, and Models*. Pasadena, CA: William Carey Library, 2003.

Hiebert, D. Edmond. *First Peter*. Chicago: Moody Press, 1984.

Hirsch, Alan. "Defining Missional." *Leadership Journal*, Fall 2008. http://www.christianitytoday.com/le/2008/fall/17.20.html.

_____. *The Forgotten Ways: Reactivating the Missional Church*. Grand Rapids: Brazos Press, 2009.

Hirsch, Alan, and Debra Hirsch. *Untamed: Reactivating a Missional Form of Discipleship*. Grand Rapids: Baker Books, 2010.

Hodges, John Mason. "Aesthetics and the Place of Beauty in Worship." *Reformation and Revival* 9, no. 3 (2000): 58–76.

Horton, Michael S. "How the Kingdom Comes." *Christianity Today* 50, no. 1 (January 2006): 42.

Howe, Frederic R. "The Christian Life in Peter's Theology." *Bibliotheca Sacra* 157, no. 627 (July 2000): 303–14.

Hughes, R. Kent. *Acts: The Church Afire*. Wheaton, IL: Crossway, 1996.

Hunsberger, George. *Bearing the Witness of the Spirit: Lesslie Newbigin's Theology of Cultural Plurality*. Grand Rapids: Wm. B. Eerdmans, 1998.

_____. *The Church Between Gospel and Culture: The Emerging Mission in North America*. Grand Rapids: Wm. B. Eerdmans, 1996.

International Missionary Council. *The Growing Church*. London: Oxford University Press, 1939.

Johansson, Calvin M. *Discipling Music Ministry: Twenty-First Century Directions*. Peabody, MA: Hendrickson Publishers, 1992.

Jones, Peter Rhea. "A Superior Life: Hebrews 12:3–13:25." *Review and Expositor* 82, no. 3 (1985): 389–402.

Juhnke, James C. *A People of Two Kingdoms: The Political Acculturation of the Kansas Mennonites*. Newton, KS: Faith & Life Press, 1975.

Kato, Byang H. "The Gospel, Cultural Context and Religious Syncretism." In *Let the Earth Hear His Voice*, edited by J. D. Douglas, 1216–23. Minneapolis: World Wide Publications, 1975.

Keller, Timothy J. "Evangelistic Worship," June 2001. http://download.redeemer.com/pdf/learn/resources/Evangelistic_Worship-Keller.pdf.

Kent, Homer. *The Epistle to the Hebrews: A Commentary*. Grand Rapids: Baker Book House, 1972.

Kilby, Clyde S. *Christianity and Aesthetics*. Chicago: Inter-Varsity Press, 1961.

Kimball, Dan. "Emerging Worship." In *Perspectives on Christian Worship: Five Views*, edited by J. Matthew Pinson, 288–333. Nashville: B&H Publishing Group, 2009.

_____. *Emerging Worship: Creating Worship Gatherings for New Generations*. Grand Rapids: Zondervan, 2009.

Kittel Gerhard, and Friedrich Gerhard, eds. *Theological Dictionary of the New Testament: Index*. Vol. 2. Grand Rapids: Wm. B. Eerdmans, 1976.

Kraft, Charles H. "Interpreting in Cultural Context." *Journal of the Evangelical Theological Society* 21, no. 4 (December 1978): 357–67.

Kuyper, Abraham. "Common Grace." In *Abraham Kuyper: A Centennial Reader*, edited by James D. Bratt. Grand Rapids: Wm. B. Eerdmans, 1998.

———. *Lectures on Calvinism*. Grand Rapids: Wm. B. Eerdmans, 1931.

———. "Sphere Sovereignty." In *Abraham Kuyper: A Centennial Reader*, edited by James D. Bratt. Grand Rapids: Wm. B. Eerdmans, 1998.

Laistner, M. L. W. *Christianity and Pagan Culture in the Later Roman Empire*. Ithaca, NY: Cornell University Press, 1979.

Lane, William. *Hebrews*. Dallas: Word Books, 1991.

Lepinski, Jon Paul. "Engaging Postmoderns in Worship: A Study of Effective Techniques and Methods Utilized by Two Growing Churches in Northern California." D.Min. thesis, Liberty Theological Seminary, 2010.

Lief, Jason. "Is Neo-Calvinism Calvinist? A Neo-Calvinist Engagement of Calvin's Two-Kingdom Doctrine." *Pro Rege* 27, no. 3 (March 2009): 1–12.

Littell, Franklin H. *The Anabaptist View of the Church*. 2nd ed., rev. and enl. Paris, AR: The Baptist Standard Bearer, 2001.

Longman III., Tremper. *How to Read the Psalms*. Downers Grove, IL: IVP Academic, 1988.

Losie, Lynn Allan. "Paul's Speech on the Areopagus: A Model of Cross-Cultural Evangelism." In *Mission in Acts: Ancient Narratives in Contemporary Context*, edited by Robert L. Gallagher and Paul Hertig, 222–39. Maryknoll, NY: Orbis Books, 2004.

Luther, Martin. "An Open Letter on the Harsh Book against the Peasants." In *Luther's Works*, edited by Robert C. Schultz and Helmut T. Lehman, 46:57–84. Philadelphia: Fortress Press, 1967.

_____. "Temporal Authority: To What Extent It Should Be Obeyed." In *Luther's Works*, edited by Walther I. Brandt and Helmut T. Lehmann, 45:75–129. Philadelphia: Muhlenberg, 1962.

Luther, Martin, and Desiderius Erasmus. *Luther and Erasmus: Free Will and Salvation.* Edited by E. Gordon Rupp and Philip S. Watson. Philadelphia: Westminster John Knox Press, 1969.

MacDonald, George. *The Imagination, and Other Essays.* Boston: D. Lothrop, 1883.

Macky, Peter W. "The Role of Metaphor in Christian Thought and Experience as Understood by Gordon Clark and C. S. Lewis." *Journal of the Evangelical Theological Society* 24, no. 3 (1981): 238–50.

Makujina, John. *Measuring the Music: Another Look at the Contemporary Christian Music Debate.* Willow Street, PA: Old Paths Publications, 2002.

Matthijssen, Jan P. "The Bern Disputation of 1538." *Mennonite Quarterly Review* 22 (January 1948): 19–33.

McKinnon, James W. *Music in Early Christian Literature.* Cambridge: Cambridge University Press, 1989.

McLoughlin, William G. *Modern Revivalism: Charles Grandison Finney to Billy Graham.* New York: Ronald Press, 1958.

McLuhan, Marshall. *Understanding Media: The Extensions of Man.* New York: McGraw-Hill, 1964.

Mead, Loren. *The Once and Future Church: Reinventing the Congregation for a New Mission Frontier.* Washington, DC: Alban Institute, 1991.

Meister, Chad V. "Truth, Evangelicalism, and the Bible." *Christian Apologetics* 5, no. 1 (2006): 107–22.

Meyers, Carol L. *The Tabernacle Menorah: A Synthetic Study of a Symbol from the Biblical Cult*. Piscataway, NJ: Gorgias Press LLC, 2003.

Moore, Jerry D. *Visions of Culture: An Introduction to Anthropological Theories and Theorists*. Lanham, MD: Rowman Altamira, 2009.

Morgenthaler, Sally. "Worship as Evangelism." *Rev! Magazine*, June 2007.

_____. *Worship Evangelism: Inviting Unbelievers into the Presence of God*. Grand Rapids: Zondervan, 1999.

Morris, Leon. "Hebrews." In *The Expositor's Bible Commentary, Hebrews–Revelation*, edited by Frank E. Gaebelein. Grand Rapids: Zondervan, 1981.

Mounce, Robert H. *The Book of Revelation*. Grand Rapids: Wm. B. Eerdmans, 1998.

Murray, John. "Common Grace." In *Collected Writings of John Murray*. Vol. 2. Carlisle, PA: Banner of Truth, 1991.

Murray, Stuart. *Post-Christendom: Church and Mission in a Strange New World*. Carlisle, PA: Paternoster, 2004.

Newbigin, Lesslie. *Foolishness to the Greeks: The Gospel and Western Culture*. Grand Rapids: Wm. B. Eerdmans, 1986.

_____. *The Other Side of 1984: Questions for the Churches*. Geneva: World Council of Churches, 1983.

Niebuhr, H. Richard. *Christ and Culture*. Harper & Row, 1975.

Paris, Jenell Williams, and Brian M. Howell. *Introducing Cultural Anthropology: A Christian Perspective*. Grand Rapids: Baker Academic, 2010.

Parris, Stanley Glenn. "Instituting a Missional Worship Style in a Local Church Developed from an Analysis of the Culture." PhD diss., Asbury Theological Seminary, 2008.

Peterson, David. *The Acts of the Apostles.* Grand Rapids: Wm. B. Eerdmans, 2009.

Pierce, Timothy M. *Enthroned on Our Praise: An Old Testament Theology of Worship.* Nashville: B&H Publishing Group, 2008.

Piper, John. *Bloodlines.* Wheaton, IL: Crossway Books, 2011.

_____. *Let the Nations Be Glad: The Supremacy of God in Missions.* 3rd ed. Grand Rapids: Baker Academic, 2010.

Plantinga, Cornelius J. *Engaging God's World: A Christian Vision of Faith, Learning, and Living.* Grand Rapids: Wm. B. Eerdmans, 2002.

Polhill, John B. *Acts.* Nashville: B&H Publishing Group, 1992.

Richardson, Cyril C., ed. "The Teaching of the Twelve Apostles, Commonly Called the Didache." In *Early Christian Fathers.* New York: Collier, 1970.

Ross, Allen. *Recalling the Hope of Glory: Biblical Worship from the Garden to the New Creation.* Grand Rapids: Kregel, 2006.

Ross, Allen P. *Holiness to the Lord: A Guide to the Exposition of the Book of Leviticus.* Grand Rapids: Baker, 2006.

Roxburgh, Alan J. "Missional Leadership: Equipping God's People for Mission." In *Missional Church: A Vision for the Sending of the Church in North America,* edited by Darrell Guder, 183–220. Grand Rapids: Wm. B. Eerdmans, 1998.

Ryken, Leland. "The Bible as Literature Part 4: 'With Many Such Parables': The Imagination as a Means of Grace." *Bibliotheca Sacra* 147, no. 587 (1990): 384–98.

Ryken, Leland, and Tremper Longman, eds. *A Complete Literary Guide to the Bible*. Grand Rapids: Zondervan, 1993.

Ryken, Phillip Graham, Derek W. H. Thomas, and J. Ligon Duncan III, eds. *Give Praise to God: A Vision for Reforming Worship, Celebrating the Legacy of James Montgomery Boice*. Phillipsburg, NJ: P & R Publishing Company, 2011.

Schattauer, Thomas H. *Inside Out: Worship in an Age of Mission*. Minneapolis: Fortress Press, 1999.

Schusky, Ernest Lester. *The Study of Cultural Anthropology*. New York: Holt, Rinehart and Winston, 1975.

Snoeberger, Mark A. "D. A. Carson's Christ and Culture Revisited: A Reflection and a Response." *Detroit Baptist Seminary Journal* 13 (2008): 93–107.

_____. "History, Ecclesiology, and Mission, Or, Are We Missing Some Options Here?" Unpublished, Detroit Baptist Theological Seminary, n.d. http://www.dbts.edu/pdf/macp/2010/Snoeberger,%20 History%20Ecclesiology%20and%20Mission.pdf.

_____. "Noetic Sin, Neutrality, and Contextualization: How Culture Receives the Gospel." *Detroit Baptist Seminary Journal* 9 (2004): 345–78.

Spiegel, James S. "Aesthetics and Worship." *Southern Baptist Journal of Theology* 2, no. 4 (1998): 38–54.

Stapert, Calvin R. *A New Song for an Old World: Musical Thought in the Early Church*. Grand Rapids: Wm. B. Eerdmans, 2006.

Stetzer, Ed. *Planting Missional Churches*. Nashville: Broadman & Holman, 2006.

Stetzer, Ed, and David Putman. *Breaking the Missional Code: Your Church Can Become a Missionary in Your Community*. Nashville: Broadman & Holman, 2006.

Stob, Henry. *Theological Reflections: Essays on Related Themes*. Grand Rapids: Wm. B. Eerdmans, 1981.

Stocking, Jr., George W. "Franz Boas and the Culture Concept in Historical Perspective." *American Anthropologist* 68 (1966): 867–82.

Stott, John R. W. *Christian Mission in the Modern World*. Downers Grove, IL: InterVarsity Press, 1975.

_____. *The Message of Acts: The Spirit, the Church, and the World (Bible Speaks Today)*. Reprint. Downers Grove, IL: InterVarsity Press, 1994.

Strong, James. *The Exhaustive Concordance of the Bible: Showing Every Word of the Text of the Common English Version of the Canonical Books, and Every Occurrence of Each Word in Regular Order, Together with Dictionaries of the Hebrew and Greek Words of the Original, with References to the English Words*. Peabody, MA: Hendrickson, 2004.

Swanson, James. *Dictionary of Biblical Languages with Semantic Domains: Greek (New Testament)*. electronic ed. Oak Harbor, WA: Logos Research Systems, Inc., 1997.

Tertullian. *The Prescription against Heretics*. Vol. 3. Ante-Nicene Fathers. Grand Rapids: Wm. B. Eerdmans, 1951.

Thernstrom, Stephan, and Abigail Thernstrom. *America in Black and White: One Nation, Indivisible*. New York: Simon & Schuster, 1999.

Thomas, Robert. *Revelation 1–7 Commentary*. Chicago: Moody Publishers, 1992.

Torrance, James. *Worship, Community, and the Triune God of Grace*. Downers Grove, IL: InterVarsity Press, 1996.

Towns, Elmer, and Edward Stetzer. *Perimeters of Light: Biblical Boundaries for the Emerging Church*. Chicago: Moody Publishers, 2004.

Tylor, Edward B. *Primitive Culture: Researches into the Development of Mythology, Philosophy, Religion, Art, and Custom*. London: John Murray, 1871.

Van Gelder, Craig. *Confident Witness—Changing World: Rediscovering the Gospel in North America*. Grand Rapids: Wm. B. Eerdmans, 1999.

_____. "Defining the Center—Finding the Boundaries." In *The Church Between Gospel and Culture: The Emerging Mission in North America*, edited by George Hunsberger and Craig Van Gelder, 26–48. Grand Rapids: Wm. B. Eerdmans, 1996.

_____. "Missional Challenge: Understanding the Church in North America." In *Missional Church: A Vision for the Sending of the Church in North America*, edited by Darrell Guder, 46–76. Grand Rapids: Wm. B. Eerdmans, 1998.

_____. "Missional Context: Understanding North American Culture." In *Missional Church: A Vision for the Sending of the Church in North America*, edited by Darrell Guder, 18–45. Grand Rapids: Wm. B. Eerdmans, 1998.

_____. *The Ministry of the Missional Church: A Community Led by the Spirit*. Grand Rapids: Baker Books, 2007.

_____. *The Missional Church and Leadership Formation: Helping Congregations Develop Leadership Capacity*. Grand Rapids: Wm. B. Eerdmans, 2009.

Van Gelder, Craig, and Dwight J. Zscheile. *The Missional Church in Perspective: Mapping Trends and Shaping the Conversation*. Grand Rapids: Baker Academic, 2011.

VanDrunen, David. *Living in God's Two Kingdoms: A Biblical Vision for Christianity and Culture*. Wheaton, IL: Crossway, 2010.

_____. *Natural Law and the Two Kingdoms: A Study in the Development of Reformed Social Thought*. Grand Rapids: Wm. B. Eerdmans, 2009.

Vanhoozer, Kevin J. "Lost in Interpretation? Truth, Scripture, and Hermeneutics." *Journal of the Evangelical Theological Society* 48, no. 1 (2005): 88–114.

_____. *The Drama of Doctrine: A Canonical-Linguistic Approach to Christian Theology*. Louisville, KY: Westminster John Knox Press, 2005.

Wells, David F. "Marketing the Church: Analysis and Assessment." *Faith and Mission* 12, no. 2 (Spring 1995): 3–20.

Wilder, Terry L. "A Biblical Theology of Mission and Contextualization." *Southwestern Journal of Theology* 55, no. 1 (Fall 2012): 3–17.

Williams, George H., and Angel M. Mergal, eds. *Spiritual and Anabaptist Writers*. Philadelphia: Westminster, 1957.

Wolters, Albert M. *Creation Regained: Biblical Basics for a Reformational Worldview*. 2nd ed. Grand Rapids: Wm. B. Eerdmans, 2005.

Wolterstorff, Nicholas. *Until Justice and Peace Embrace: The Kuyper Lectures for 1981 Delivered at the Free University of Amsterdam*. Grand Rapids: Wm. B. Eerdmans, 1983.

Wright, Christopher. *The Mission of God: Unlocking the Bible's Grand Narrative*. Downers Grove, IL: IVP Academic, 2006.

Wright, David F. "A Race Apart? Jews, Gentiles, Christians." *Bibliotheca Sacra* 160, no. 368 (April 2003): 132–40.

Yarnell III, Malcolm B. "Global Choices for Twenty-First Century Christians: Bringing Clarity to Missional Theology." *Southwestern Journal of Theology* 55, no. 1 (Fall 2012): 18–36.

"Your Kingdom Come." a pamphlet published by the World Conference on Mission and Evangelism, n.d.

SCRIPTURE INDEX

SUBJECT INDEX